# 1 Introduction

The financial crisis of 2007–09 has spurred considerable debate over the role deregulation played in the instability of the financial system. One particular area of interest has been the treatment of derivatives and repurchase agreements (repos) in bankruptcy. For the most part, when firms in the United States file for bankruptcy, a temporary hold is placed on the their assets known as *automatic stay*. The logic behind this bankruptcy provision is to prohibit creditors from collecting payments in a disorderly fashion, maintaining the firm as a going concern.[1] This provision does not exist for derivatives and repos, which are exempt from automatic stay. Counterparties to these contracts have, among other things, immediate access to any collateral posted by the defaulted party. This is particularly important for repo contracts, which in essence are secured loans backed by financial assets. The consequences of repo's exemption from stay is a relatively broad research question, and this paper focuses on a particular aspect of the debate, namely the impact of *fire sales* stemming from repo's special treatment on firms' incentives ex ante.

This paper addresses the issue by examining agents' financing and investment decisions under two regulatory regimes: repo subject to, or exempt from, automatic stay. The model features a continuum of firms with limited capital that raise debt from a competitive lending sector to purchase a risky asset. In the stay regime, in case of a debtor's default, secured lenders (i.e., repo lenders) must wait until the following period to receive their collateral. In the stay exemption regime, repo lenders have immediate access to the contract's collateral and have incentives to sell it to surviving firms, causing a fire sale. Fire sales occur because of solvent firms' limited capacity to purchase assets after a default event — a *cash-in-the-market* style pricing. Thus, repo's exemption from stay alters firms' investment opportunity set, potentially giving them the opportunity to purchase assets at discounted prices in the future. This opportunity creates incentives for firms to hold on to their initial cash endowment (*dry powder*), placing a premium on liquidity and reducing demand for the risky asset.

Specifically, in the stay exemption regime, firms' incentives to exploit future fire sales attracts capital that would have otherwise participated in the market initially, thereby reducing initial asset demand and consequently its price before the fire sale. Firms' incentives to use their liquidity in the future places more assets in the hands of firms with preferences to take large positions and risk default, which is assumed to be costly. Moreover, the initial price discount can be so severe, that even firms that do not have preferences to become large are motivated to choose high levels of debt, increasing the fraction of defaulting firms in the economy. This is not the case when repo is subject to automatic stay, since the lock-up of secured lenders' collateral doesn't allow its immediate sale after default, effectively eliminating any possibility of a fire sale.

---

[1]For the history of automatic stays in U.S. bankruptcy, see Skeel (2001).

The base setup consists of a group of firms — interpreted as dealer banks, hedge funds, or commercial banks — endowed with a fixed initial capital stock that raise debt from a competitive lending sector — interpreted as money market funds and bond investors — to purchase a risky asset. Because of reasons outside the model, a fixed fraction of firms enjoy *private benefits* for holding large risky asset positions, inducing them to take on higher leverage. This modeling device captures the fact that many financial firms increase their asset size by taking on debt, and that there is heterogeneity in financial firms' leverage.[2] Therefore, the number of assets each firm can purchase depends on its initial endowment, the amount of debt it can raise, and its willingness to take on default risk. A well-capitalized lending market offers secured and unsecured loans to firms, where secured contracts set aside a fraction of the firm's risky asset position as collateral (i.e., repo contract). Firms are constrained as to how much debt they can raise, either because of regulatory constraints or because the lending sector demands them to have some participation in their portfolio's outcome. It is assumed that there are direct bankruptcy costs that must be paid from the firms' assets, making default costly, which lenders price accordingly.

The main difference between regimes is that when repo is exempt from stay, secured lenders have access to the asset and sell it immediately to the remaining solvent firms. This assumption is paramount to the model but is easily motivated. Currently many of the lenders participating in repo markets cannot hold long-dated assets because of regulatory restrictions or lack of expertise (e.g., money market funds), giving them strong incentives to sell it in case of default. Moreover, conditional on having to sell, the lender has limited incentives to find a "good" trading price since once the repo lender is made whole, any additional upside on the collateral is the property of the borrower.[3] Thus, the lender's upside is bounded by the face value of the loan, but its downside may be substantial. For simplicity, in the model I assumed that repo contracts are overcollateralized to such an extent that the loan is absolutely safe.[4] This particular contracting feature eliminates any incentive for the lender to hold the asset after the borrower defaults, making the asset supply insensitive to the fire sale. Therefore, in a default event, the asset's market clearing price will depend on solvent firms' ability to raise funds and defaulting firms' initial asset holdings, potentially creating a price below the asset's expected future payoff.

An important element of the model is the lack of initial capital committed to the market. This lack is due to market segmentation that only allows a fixed set of firms with limited capital to participate in the market. Market segmentation can arise because of a specific expertise needed to trade in the risky asset market, which only a limited number of firms possess. This segmentation also implies that more capital does not flood into the market after firms default, which could result from an unmodeled lemons problem that

---

[2]Adrian et al. (2012) and He et al. (2010) present evidence of this during the 2007–09 financial crisis.

[3]This contracting feature is present in standard Master Repurchase Agreements.

[4]This assumption is in line with the notion that repo loans are "relatively safe."

outside investors suffer by participating in a market unfamiliar to them. Potentially because of slow moving capital, it takes time for new investors to come into the market, leaving only the original participants to take advantage of the price discount.[5]

Because of firms' incentives to wait for future price dislocations, the stay exemption regime produces higher default costs since more assets are in the hands of firms that risk default. This paper also explores potential policy prescriptions that, in the context of the model, would eliminate the fire sale in the stay exemption regime, namely an asset purchase program by the government or a contracting change to repo arrangements. A brief subsection is dedicated to an environment where agents do not internalize the future cash-in-the-market pricing, which increases uncertainty and the magnitude of the fire sale, and potentially puts more firms at risk of default. Since firms' debt capacity depends on the value of their portfolio, unforeseen price reductions could hinder their ability to roll over their debt, putting their solvency into question.

This paper is inspired by the events that unfolded during the 2007–09 financial crisis. During that time, policy makers were concerned that fire sales could arise in relatively illiquid markets, for example the mortgage-backed securities (MBS) market, having destabilizing effects. The paper provides anecdotal evidence pointing to the main mechanism of the model, namely the unwillingness of market participants to purchase assets initially in anticipation of further market disruptions. These disruptions were plausible given the current regulatory regime that would have liberated illiquid repo collateral after a default event.

The rest of the paper is structured as follows. The following section presents a literature review, with a brief overview of the current debate over derivatives' and repos' exemption from automatic stay. Section 3 introduces the model setup, detailing the main market frictions driving the results. Section 4 presents firms' optimal strategies, and Section 5 characterizes the resulting equilibrium in both regulatory regimes. Having detailed the model's mechanics, Section 6 goes back to the stay versus stay exemption debate to put the model into context with the existing literature, highlighting the types of markets that this paper is most relevant to and giving anecdotal evidence for the model's main mechanism. Section 7 presents the cost–benefit analysis, some policy considerations, and extensions to the original model. The final section concludes.

## 2  Related Literature

The question as to whether the exclusion of repos from normal bankruptcy proceedings can have an impact on the stability of the financial system has interested economic and law scholars alike. Skeel and Jackson

---

[5]See Duffie (2010).

(2012) provide a detailed account of the rationale behind exempting repo from automatic stay, which was to mitigate the possibility of a run given the contract's easy resolution in bankruptcy. They argue that during the 2008 crisis repo's exemption played a minor role in preventing runs, and in fact aggravated troubled firms situation by not providing the regular protections enjoyed under bankruptcy. More broadly, Duffie and Skeel (2012) provide a detailed discussion of the role of stay exemption and the main trade offs in the debate.

A rigorous economic analysis of the ex ante effect of stay exemption is given by Bolton and Oehmke (2011) in the context of firms engaging in derivative contracts to hedge part of their operational risk. They show that stay exemption creates incentives for firms to shift risk from derivative counterparties to debt holders, and the desirability of automatic stay exemption depends on which one of these agents can bear default risk more efficiently. If it is more costly for debt holders to bear the risks associated with default, then the stay exemption is undesirable. In this paper, I study the ex ante effects of repo's stay exemption as a funding vehicle and analyze how different bankruptcy regimes can change firms' aggregate risk-taking, which has an effect on asset prices.

Specifically, this paper studies a particular externality that could arise from a mass default event that would induce an asset sell off and a dramatic reduction in prices, i.e., a fire sale.[6] Stein (2012) studies the ex post effect of fire sales, which attract capital that could have been used more efficiently in other investment projects. Antinolfi et al. (2012) take this view in the context of repo stay exemption, where the optimal bankruptcy regime balances the reduction in capital to productive investment because of a fire sale, with lenders' preference for immediacy. Acharya et al. (2011) and Diamond and Rajan (2011) study a mechanism similar to the one presented in this paper: future fire sales that create incentives to hoard liquidity ex ante. Though the focus of this paper is to study how the bankruptcy treatment of a specific lending contract affects firms' investment decisions, which impact the severity of price dislocations, the level of leverage in the economy, and the amount of default risk in the economy. An extension of the model will also explore an additional fire sale externality: the reduction of firms' debt capacity that could propagate defaults.[7]

This paper is also related to the vast literature on capital constraints and their effects on prices, from the original paper by Kiyotaki and Moore (1997) where hard collateral constraints limit agents' funding, to the more recent literature that studies how different manifestations of capital constraints can influence intermediaries decisions (for example, Gromb and Vayanos (2002), Brunnermeier and Pedersen (2009), He and Krishnamurthy (2012), and Krishnamurthy (2010)). The recurring theme is how particular balance sheet

---

[6] One mechanism behind fire sales is when high-valuation agents are forced to sell assets to low-valuation buyers (for example Shleifer and Vishny (1992), (1997)). In this paper, fire sales arise because of market segmentation and agents' limited capital to increase demand. Shleifer and Vishny (2011) provide a complete overview of the existing fire sale literature.

[7] See Stein (2013) for a discussion on how fire sales can hinder firms' financing.

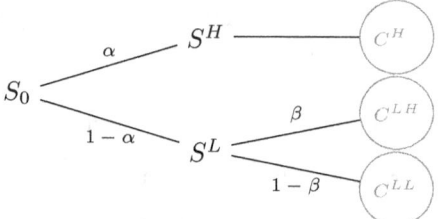

**Figure 1:** Risky asset process

constraints affect the capacity of intermediaries to trade assets, limiting their ability to exploit arbitrage opportunities and allowing prices to deviate from fundamentals. This is related to the intuition introduced by Allen and Gale (1994), (1998), and (2005) referred to as "cash-in-the-market" pricing, which illustrates how limited demand can cause an asset's price to be lower than its fundamental. These mechanisms are key in this paper since firms face limits on the amount of debt they can raise that depend on the value of their portfolio, which ultimately affects their demand.

# 3    Model Set Up

The model consists of three periods $t \in \{0, 1, 2\}$, where specialized firms raise one period debt from a competitive lending sector to finance their position in a single risky asset. Firms avoid default if the amount of cash they receive from the asset, or from additional funding, is sufficient to pay off existing creditors. The model is analyzed under two distinct regulatory regimes: repo subject to automatic stay (regime $\mathcal{S}$) or repo exempt from automatic stay (regime $\mathcal{SE}$).

## 3.1    Assets

There is an initial fixed supply $K$ of one risky asset, which produces three possible cash flows in the final period: $\{C^H, C^{LH}, C^{LL}\}$, with $C^H > C^{LH} > C^{LL}$. After period zero with probability $\alpha$, the asset has a high outcome and will pay a cash flow of $C^H$ for sure in $t = 2$. With probability $1 - \alpha$, the asset has a low outcome and still has some residual uncertainty: With probability $\beta$, it will pay off $C^{LH}$, and with probability $1 - \beta$, it will payoff $C^{LL}$. Thus, after a low outcome, the expected future cash flow of the asset is denoted by $C^L = \beta C^{LH} + (1 - \beta)C^{LL}$. The initial expected cash flow of the asset is denoted by $\overline{C} = \alpha C^H + (1 - \alpha)C^L$. The initial market clearing price for the asset is denoted by $S$, and in period 1 the price is denoted by $S^H$ or $S^L$ in the high and low state, respectively (see Figure 1). There is also a numéraire safe asset called "cash" and a storage technology to deposit it in with a gross interest rate normalized to 1.

## 3.2 Agents

There are a continuum of risk-neutral firms who have an initial cash endowment $A^I$ and raise funds from a competitive lending sector to finance their risky asset position $Q$. Firms are the only agents in the economy that can buy and hold the risky asset. They are risk neutral, but a fraction $\theta$ also enjoy private benefits $b$ proportional to the size of their initial risky asset position. Private benefits can be interpreted as perks that firm managers enjoy for holding large risky asset positions, an unmodeled convenience yield perceived by these firms proportional to the portfolio size[8] or optimism in the final cash flow of the asset.[9] The nature of these private benefits is not important. In essence, it is a modeling device to ensure that some firms have incentives to increase their risky asset position by taking on risky debt that will be assumed to be costly.[10] Firms that receive private benefits are referred to as "private benefit firms". The aggregate demand of private-benefit and non private benefit firms at time $t$ are denoted by $\overline{Q}_t^{PB}$ and $\overline{Q}_t^{NPB}$, respectively.

Lenders are risk neutral, and their role is to provide firms with cash to increase their portfolio size. They have unlimited access to funds but cannot invest in the risky asset directly. That is, they can only gain exposure to the risky asset by lending to firms (i.e., market segmentation). This segmentation can be motivated by a prior participation decision that gave firms the expertise to trade in said risky asset market. Lenders can invest in two possible debt contracts: secured and unsecured. Secured debt, interpreted as repos, earmarks a fraction of the firms risky portfolio as collateral, which lenders have first lien on in case of default. Unsecured debt have a claim to the firm's remaining assets.[11]

Note that market segmentation plays two important roles. First, it makes the market clearing price depend on firms' ability to raise funds, inducing cash-in-the-market pricing. Second, when repo is exempt from automatic stay, market segmentation makes secured lenders' supply of the asset insensitive to the market clearing price. This outcome is aggravated further since conditional on wanting to sell, lenders have little incentive to react to a low trading price since any gain above and beyond the promised debt payment is property of the original borrower.[12]

## 3.3 Firm Liabilities

Lenders use one-period secured and unsecured debt to satisfy firms' demand for funds. Secured lending contracts are assumed to be absolutely safe, thus the loan repayment must be covered by the worst possible out-

---

[8]For example, through market making for the risky asset.

[9]These firms may believe the high asset outcome will be $\hat{C}^H$ with $\hat{C}^H - C^H = \frac{b}{\alpha}$, and agree to disagree with other agents in the economy. In this setting, if the asset has a high payoff these firms update their beliefs, eliminating their optimism for the final period.

[10]Details on default costs are in subsection 3.4.

[11]Details on debt contracts are in subsection 3.3.

[12]Oehmke (2013) studies the problem faced by agents attempting to sell defaulted collateral in an illiquid market.

come of the asset (i.e., fully collateralized). This assumption avoids having to determine the haircut/interest rate trade off, simplifying the terms of trade between repo lenders and borrowers.[13] Alternatively, it could be assumed that lenders purchasing secured contracts are relatively more risk averse and it's in the borrower's best interest to offer safe loans. Given a fire sale in the stay exemption regime, this assumption implies that the initial amount of secured funding a firm can raise will differ under the two regulatory regimes.

The nature of firms' default costs, elaborated in subsection 3.4, will make firms prefer secured funding before they take on any unsecured debt. Thus, to simplify firms' liability structure, I assume an exogenous upper bound on the fraction of the risky asset portfolio that can be earmarked to secured lenders $\overline{\varphi}$.[14] This eliminates the unrealistic outcome of having the entire portfolio financed by repo. Labeling $\varphi$ the fraction of the portfolio earmarked for secured lending and $P^i$ as the worst-case outcome per unit of risky asset (which depends on regime $i \in \{\mathcal{S}, \mathcal{SE}\}$), the initial secured loan amount and repayment are both

$$\varphi P^i Q$$

where $Q$ is the total quantity of risky assets held by the firm. Unsecured lenders set their lending terms to break even each period, internalizing secured lenders' priority on earmarked assets and any potential deadweight loss. This additional funding channel allows intermediaries to increase their debt capacity, taking on positions that could make them insolvent in the following period. Denoting $I^u$ the initial loan amount of unsecured funding, $F^u$ the promised payment in the next period, $D^i$ the per unit value of the firm's risky portfolio in case of default, and $1 - \lambda < 1$ the deadweight loss from liquidating any remaining fraction of the firm's endowment, lenders solve for $F^u$ using

$$I^u = \mathbb{P}(\text{no default})F^u + (1 - \mathbb{P}(\text{no default}))\left(D^i Q + \lambda A - \varphi P^i Q\right), \tag{1}$$

where $A$ and $Q$ are the amount of cash and risky assets held by the firm, respectively.[15] Thus, given the firm's choice of $\{Q, A, I^u, \varphi\}$, unsecured lenders choose $F^u$ according to equation (1). Firms default if the amount of cash on hand — either by raising new funds from the lending sector or directly from their own holdings — is not enough to pay off existing creditors.

---

[13]Martin et al. (2012) adopt a similar assumption for repo transactions, and in the framework of Geanakoplos (2010) the safe debt contract is the only one traded in equilibrium. Fostel and Geanakoplos (2011) show general conditions in which the safe contract arises and highlights the literature linking leverage and asset prices that assumes the use of the safe contract. In the context of repos, Infante (2013) shows that borrowers with a relatively large initial endowment accept contracts with haircuts that make lending risk free. This finding is in line with the notion that repo loans are "relatively" safe investments.

[14]In a more general setup, where a firm's risky portfolio is more diverse, there may be more reasons why firms may not want to use all of their financial assets as repo collateral. For example, the expected fire sale for some asset classes may be too severe in the stay exemption regime, which limits the desire to use repo altogether.

[15]To ensure there is enough value in the firm's portfolio to make secured creditors whole $D^i Q + \lambda A - \varphi P^i Q$ must be non-negative. This is not a restrictive condition since $P^i$ is set to the asset's worst outcome and $\varphi < 1$. It ensures there is always enough value in the portfolio to pay off repo lenders.

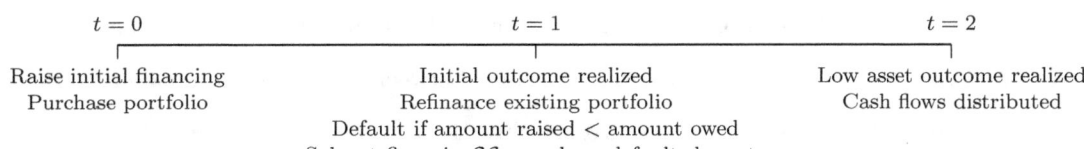

**Figure 2:** Timeline under both regimes

The model also incorporates capital constraints that limit the amount of leverage firms can adopt. This constraint can be interpreted as firms' capital requirements, or an unmodeled "skin-in-the-game" constraint to ensure that firms behave in the lender's best interests.[16] Capital constraints eliminate the possibility for a firm to turn over its entire portfolio to lenders — that is, it restricts the issuance of equity contracts. If firms were able to raise equity, the unconstrained lending sector would be able to provide enough capital for firms to eliminate any price deviation below fundamentals.[17] In the model, capital requirements at time $t$ take the form,

$$I^u + \varphi P^i Q \leq \eta (S^i Q + A), \tag{2}$$

where $\eta \in (0,1)$ is the capital requirement parameter and $S^i$ is the period $t$ market clearing price, which depends on regime $i$. Restriction (2) forces firms' equity to be at least $1 - \eta$ the market value of the firms' assets. Note that a lower asset price decreases the amount of financing firms can raise.

## 3.4 Stay vs. Stay Exemption: Timing & Defaults

The strategies and timing of the three-period model depend on which regime is under consideration. The resolution of default in period 1 is the main difference between regimes. In the stay exemption regime, a market for defaulted collateral opens where secured lenders who receive collateral sell it to solvent firms. In the stay regime, secured lenders must wait until the final period to receive their payment. The exact timing of the model under both regimes can be summarized in Figure 2.

The nature of firms' default costs are specifically related to direct costs of default. They represent the costs of litigation (experts, lawyers, etc.) to resolve disputes among claimants of a defaulted firm, which must be paid from the firms' assets.[18] It is important to characterize how these default costs affect firms under different regimes. In the stay exemption regime, collateralized assets leave the firm immediately, thus

---

[16] Although the nature of this bad behavior isn't specified, this type of friction has been commonly used in the literature. For example see Acharya et al. (2011) and Acharya and Skeie (2011).

[17] In fact, without the constraints firms that enjoy private benefits may have incentives to raise funding beyond the default value of the portfolio, potentially increasing the initial price beyond it's fundamental value.

[18] They are not indirect costs due to the suboptimal use of an asset by a third party, nor are they costs associated to the firm as a going concern. In the model, there is no scope to restructure the firm since in the final period all uncertainty is resolved, the asset matures, and cash flows are distributed.

it can be argued that the cost to resolve these claims are relatively small.[19] This outcome might not be the case for secured lenders in a stay regime, where disputes between various secured claimants as to which specific asset they are entitled to could arise. To simplify the comparison between regulatory regimes, I assumed that secured claims are resolved at no cost across both of them.[20]

The consequence of this assumption is that secured funding will always be preferred in the stay regime since it induces lower default costs. This will also be true in the stay exemption regime as long as $S^L \geq \lambda C^L$, which creates a natural lower bound for the fire sale. In case the fire sale price were below the defaulted value of the asset, firms that take on risky positions would not be inclined to take on secured debt, leaving only unsecured debt holders and eliminating the fire sale altogether.

To simplify the analysis, I assumed there were no default costs in the final period. This dramatically reduces the number of cases to analyze in each regime since solvent firms refinancing problem becomes trivial: in case of a fire sale, purchase as much of the asset as possible. No default costs in the final period can be motivated by assuming that it is less costly to resolve the bankruptcy of a firm with assets "closer to maturity" or alternatively that the capital requirement bound is so strict that in the final period only safe debt can be raised (i.e., $\eta C^L < C^{LL}$).[21] Knowing firms' portfolio values and default costs under both regulatory regimes, their initial debt contracts are detailed in the following subsections.

### 3.4.1 Stay Regime

In period 1 if a firm defaults, its claimants receive their payoff in the final period making the worst possible asset value $C^{LL}$. Therefore, in period 0 if a risky firm decides to purchase $Q_0$ risky assets, leave $A_0^I - A_0$ in cash, raise $\varphi_0 C^{LL} Q_0$ in secured funding, and raise $I_0^u$ in unsecured funds; period 0 unsecured lenders choose $F_0^u$ from

$$I_0^u = \alpha F_0^u + (1 - \alpha) \left( D^{\mathcal{S}}(\varphi_0) Q_0 + \lambda (A_0^I - A_0) - \varphi_0 C^{LL} Q_0 \right), \tag{3}$$

where the default value per unit of risky asset is

$$D^{\mathcal{S}}(\varphi_0) = \varphi_0 C^L + \lambda (1 - \varphi_0) C^L.$$

Since there is no market for defaulted collateral, the asset price is set to reflect fundamental value, which eliminates incentives for solvent firms to trade.

---

[19]Similar to leases in the context of Eisfeldt and Rampini (2009).

[20]An additional cost for secured assets locked in bankruptcy in the stay regime can be incorporated. This does not change any qualitative features of firms optimal strategies, nor the resulting equilibrium; it only introduces an additional parameter in the cost benefit analysis making the comparison between regimes more cumbersome. See Section 7 for more details.

[21]Both of these interpretations can be seen as two extreme cases that will impact the severity of the fire sale: easy resolution of mature assets increases debt capacity mitigating the cash-in-the-market discount; or strict capital requirements limit funding, reducing demand, and amplifying any mispricing.

### 3.4.2  Stay Exemption Regime

In period 1 if a firm defaults, secured creditors receive the asset and sell it immediately, implying that the worst possible asset value is $S^L$. Therefore, in period 0 if a risky firm decides to purchase $Q_0$ risky assets, leave $A_0^I - A_0$ in cash, raise $\varphi_0 S^L Q_0$ in secured funding, and raise $I_0^u$ in unsecured funds; period 0 unsecured lenders choose $F_0^u$ from

$$I_0^u = \alpha F_0^u + (1 - \alpha) \left( D^{\mathcal{SE}}(\varphi_0, S^L) Q_0 + \lambda(A_0^I - A_0) - \varphi_0 S^L Q_0 \right), \tag{4}$$

where the default value per unit of risky asset is

$$D^{\mathcal{SE}}(\varphi_0, S^L) = \varphi_0 S^L + \lambda(1 - \varphi_0) C^L.$$

Upon default $\varphi S^L Q_0$ go to secured creditors, leaving the remaining assets to bear the direct costs of default, which are resolved in the following period.

## 4  Firm's Optimal Strategies

In each period solvent firms must decide how much debt to raise to refinance their existing risky asset position and potentially finance a new asset purchase. This section characterizes the problem firms face and under what conditions they choose positions that may lead them to default (labeled *risky firms*), or avoid it altogether (labeled *safe firms*). It is important to note that there's no difference between secured and unsecured debt if a firm's leverage doesn't put it at risk of default. Since there is neither a concern about a safe firm's bankruptcy cost nor a change in the supply of defaulted collateral, unsecured and secured debt will turn out to be equivalent. All proofs are relegated to the appendix.

In addition, the refinancing problem in case of a high outcome in period 1 is straightforward. Firms do not default, and there is no open market for defaulted collateral, nor do private benefit firms have incentives to purchase the asset from nondefaulting firms since they only enjoy $b$ in the initial period.[22] All firms are able to refinance their portfolio making the problem trivial. Thus, all discussions and characterizations of firms' optimal strategies in period 1 were assumed to be after a low outcome in the initial period. For generality, the analysis was done from the perspective of a firm that enjoys private benefits. Strategies and payoffs for firms that do not enjoy private benefits were given by the general set up with $b = 0$.

---

[22]In this case the price equals the final cash flow, $S^H = C^H$, thus there is no incentive to trade.

## 4.1 Stay Regime

The analysis of the stay regime is relatively simple. In period 1 there is no open market to purchase defaulted collateral, thus surviving firms only need to decide how much debt to raise to pay previous creditors, i.e., roll over their debt. Conditional on the firm's current balance sheet $(Q_0, A^I - A_0, F_0)$, where $Q_0$ is the initial period's risky asset position, $A^I - A_0$ the remaining dry powder, and $F_0$ the total amount of debt to be paid in period 1, the firm must decide how much to raise to pay off $F_0$. The firm is restricted to raise new debt up to its capital requirement, and may also use its remaining dry powder to pay off its previous debt. Since there are no default costs in the final period, the firm is willing to maximize its debt capacity, which is done by taking on debt and exhausting any remaining dry powder. Therefore, the firms will be able to avoid default in period $t = 1$ if

$$F_0 \leq \eta C^L Q_0 + A^I - A_0. \tag{5}$$

Having the default condition in the refinancing period one can postulate the firm's initial financing decision. Firms have the choice to take on small levels of debt that will allow them to refinance their position in $t = 1$ (safe firms), or they can maximize their debt capacity risking default in $t = 1$ (risky firms). In case a firm decides to become risky, lenders charge a higher interest rate on the loan. Therefore, using lenders' debt pricing equation (3) to get the appropriate expression for $F_0$, firms' payoff under both strategies can be characterized. Given the size of firms' risky asset position, the amount of secured and unsecured debt, and the amount of dry powder committed purchase the risky asset, firms have the following possible payoffs:[23]

$$
\begin{aligned}
\pi^S(Q_0, A_0, I_0^u, \varphi_0; A^I, b) &= \overline{C} Q_0 + A^I - A_0 - \varphi_0 C^{LL} Q_0 - I_0^u + b Q_0, \\
\pi^R(Q_0, A_0, I_0^u, \varphi_0; A^I, b) &= \underbrace{\left[ \alpha C^H + (1-\alpha)(\varphi_0 C^L + (1-\varphi_0)\lambda C^L) \right]}_{:= C^D(\varphi_0)} Q_0 + \\
&\quad (\alpha + (1-\alpha)\lambda)(A^I - A_0) - \varphi_0 C^{LL} Q_0 - I_0^u + b Q_0.
\end{aligned}
$$

Using equation (5) I define the no default set for this regime: $N^S = \{(Q_0, A_0, I_0^u, \varphi_0) : I_0^u + \varphi_0 C^{LL} Q_0 \leq \eta C^L Q_0 + A^I - A_0\}$ that characterizes the portfolios that can roll over their debt. Thus, firms must solve the following optimization problem,[24]

$$\max_{\{Q_0, A_0, I_0^u, \varphi_0\}} \pi^S(Q_0, I_0^u, \varphi_0, A_0) \mathbf{1}_{\{(Q_0, A_0, I_0^u, \varphi_0) \in N^S\}} + \pi^R(Q_0, I_0^u, \varphi_0, A_0) \mathbf{1}_{\{(Q_0, A_0, I_0^u, \varphi_0) \in (N^S)^c\}}$$

---

[23]Details are in the appendix

[24]In the interest of brevity, I shall omit the utility function's dependence on primitive parameters $A^I$ and $b$.

subject to,

$$A_0 \leq A^I \qquad \text{Dry Powder}$$

$$SQ_0 \leq \varphi_0 C^{LL} Q_0 + I_0^u + A_0 \qquad \text{Budget}$$

$$I_0^u + \varphi_0 C^{LL} Q_0 \leq \eta(SQ_0 + (A^I - A_0)) \qquad \text{Capital Requirement}$$

$$I_0^u, A_0, Q_0 \geq 0, \ \varphi_0 \in [0, \overline{\varphi}].$$

Conditional on being safe or risky, the firm is the residual claim holder of the portfolio plus any additional private benefits it may perceive.[25] The first restriction limits the amount of cash the firm can use to purchase the asset. The second restriction is the firm's budget constraint, i.e., the amount it raises from lenders plus the amount of dry powder used must be enough to purchase the risky asset portfolio. The third restriction is the firm's capital requirement.

In this regime a firm's decision to become risky or safe depends on the size of its private benefits. Firms that have large private benefits would be willing to pay for their expected default costs to maximize their asset holdings and enjoy more of said rewards. To ensure that firms which adopt risky strategies actually default after a low asset outcome, firms' initial capital requirements can't be too restrictive. In effect, for low values of $\eta$ firms would be unable to increase their debt capacity to violate inequality (5), thus I assume

**Assumption A1.** *The capital requirement restriction $\eta$ is larger than the defaulted value of the firm: $\eta \geq \varphi_0 + \lambda(1 - \varphi_0)$.*

Assumption A1 states that the maximum amount the firm can raise is larger than the default value of the asset. The solution to the firm's initial financing problem in this regime is

**Proposition 1.** *In the stay regime if $S > C^L$ and A1 holds, there exists a function $b^*(S)$ such that if $b < b^*(S)$ the solution to the firm's initial financing problem is*

$$Q_0^* = \begin{cases} 0 & \text{if } S > \overline{C} + b \\ Q_0^{undet} & \text{if } S = \overline{C} + b \\ \frac{A^I}{S - \eta C^L} & \text{if } S < \overline{C} + b, \end{cases}$$

*where $Q_0^{undet}$ may take any value between $\left[0, \frac{A^I}{\overline{C} + b - \eta C^L}\right)$. If $b \geq b^*(S)$ the solution to the firms initial financing problem is*

$$Q_0^* = \frac{A^I}{S(1 - \eta)}.$$

---

[25]Conditional on being safe or risky the firms' optimization problem is very similar to the variable investment model of Holmstrom and Tirole (1997).

13

*These strategies lead to the following payoffs:*

$$\pi_0(S;b) = \begin{cases} A^I & \text{if } S \geq \overline{C} + b \text{ and } b < b^*(S) \\ \frac{(\overline{C}+b-S)A^I}{S-\eta C^L} + A^I & \text{if } S < \overline{C} + b \text{ and } b < b^*(S) \\ \frac{(C^D(\overline{\varphi})+b-S)A^I}{S(1-\eta)} + A^I & \text{if } b \geq b^*(S). \end{cases}$$

The solution to the firm's investment and financing problem can be split in two. Conditional on the decision to become safe or risky, the firm's problem is linear. For relatively large private benefits firms will prefer to maximize their risky asset position, assuming the cost of potential default. For relatively low private benefits, firms take a safe strategy where they either retain their dry powder, raise debt up to their refinancing condition, or are indifferent between these strategies. The price at which safe firms are indifferent is called the *breakeven price*, which in this case is equal to $\overline{C} + b$. The function $b^*(S)$ characterizes for what prices firms decide to take on safe or risky strategies, which ultimately pins down the amount of default in the economy.[26]

## 4.2 Stay Exemption Regime

In this regime, firms must internalize the possibility of an open market after a low outcome. Surviving firms not only have to refinance their existing portfolios but must also raise additional funds to purchase defaulted collateral. As noted earlier, the price for the defaulted asset may be lower than the expected value of its future cash flows due to limited demand. The potential price discount has two effects: first it generates a profit for nondefaulting firms, creating incentives to underinvest in the initial period. Second, because of mark-to-market pricing, firms' capital requirements limit their ability to raise debt, which aggravates the price discount. The focus of the model will be in a context where $S^L \leq C^L$, and a fire sale is said to occur when the inequality is strict.

Since there are no default costs in the final period, in period 1 if the asset price is below its expected future cash flow, firms will want to maximize their debt capacity and make as many new purchases as possible, i.e., maximize $Q_1$. This will be restricted by their period 1 capital requirements. Therefore, for $S^L < C^L$ firms will solve,

$$S^L Q_1 = \varphi_1 C^{LL}(Q_0 + Q_1) + I_1^u + A^I - A_0 - F_0,$$

$$I_1^u + \varphi_1 C^{LL}(Q_0 + Q_1) = \eta S^L (Q_0 + Q_1),$$

where the first equality is the firm's budget constraint and the second is its capital requirement restriction.

---

[26]See appendix for details.

14

Firms raise secured funding earmarking their existing and new asset holdings, and also raise unsecured debt. As in the stay regime, it is optimal for the firm to exhaust its remaining dry powder to maximize the asset purchase. Therefore, in case of a fire sale a firm's asset purchase in $t = 1$ is

$$Q_1^* = \frac{\eta S^L Q_0 + A^I - A_0 - F_0}{S^L(1-\eta)}. \tag{6}$$

Note that $Q_1^* < 0$ implies the firm is unable to pay off existing creditors and therefore must default. In case $S^L = C^L$, firms will have no incentive to purchase the asset, and their $t = 1$ demand is undetermined. A firm with $(Q_0, A^I - A_0, F_0)$ that can roll over its debt gets the following expected payoff when refinancing:

$$\pi_1(Q_0, A^I - A_0, F_0; b) = \begin{cases} C^L Q_0 + A^I - A_0 - F_0 & \text{if } S^L = C^L \\ C^L Q_0 + A^I - A_0 - F_0 + (C^L - S^L)Q_1^* & \text{if } S^L < C^L. \end{cases}$$

Having the firm's optimal asset choice, and refinancing condition in $t = 1$, one can postulate the firm's initial financing decision. Similar to the stay regime, firms have the choice between taking on small levels of debt that allow them to refinance their position in $t = 1$ (safe firms), or they can maximize their debt capacity, risking default (risky firms). Though in this regime safe firms internalize that if they use too much of their debt capacity in the initial period, they will reduce their ability to purchase defaulted collateral in the future. Specifically, if they expect a large price discount in the refinancing period it may be optimal to withhold their initial dry powder rather than participate in the initial market.

Using the firm's payoff in the refinancing period, and lenders debt pricing equation (4) to get the appropriate expression for $F_0$, firms' payoff under both strategies can be characterized. In effect, given the firm's asset position, its initial debt structure, and the amount of dry powder committed to the initial purchase, the firm's expected payoffs are expressed as:[27]

$$\begin{aligned} \pi^S(Q_0, , A_0, I_0^u, \varphi_0; A^I, b, S^L) &= \overline{C}Q_0 + A^I - A_0 + \\ &\quad (1-\alpha)(C^L - S^L)\left(\frac{\eta S^L Q_0 + A^I - A_0 - \varphi_0 S^L Q_0 - I_0^u}{S^L(1-\eta)}\right) - \\ &\quad \varphi_0 S^L Q_0 - I_0^u + bQ_0, \\ \pi^R(Q_0, A_0, I_0^u, \varphi_0; A^I, b, S^L) &= \underbrace{\left[\alpha C^H + (1-\alpha)(\varphi_0 S^L + (1-\varphi_0)\lambda C^L)\right]}_{:=C^D(\varphi_0, S^L)} Q_0 + \\ &\quad (\alpha + (1-\alpha)\lambda)(A^I - A_0) - \varphi_0 S^L Q_0 - I_0^u + bQ_0. \end{aligned}$$

From equation (6), the firm's default condition can be deduced (whenever $Q_1^* < 0$), and I can define

---

[27]Details are in the appendix.

the no-default set for this regime: $N^{S\mathcal{E}} = \{(Q_0, A_0, I_0^u, \varphi_0) : I_0^u + \varphi_0 S^L Q_0 \leq \eta S^L Q_0 + A^I - A_0\}$ that characterizes the portfolios that can roll over their debt in $t = 1$, which depends on $S^L$. This gives the following optimization problem for $t = 0$, [28]

$$\max_{\{Q_0, \varphi_0, I_0^u, A_0\}} \pi^S(Q_0, I_0^u, \varphi_0, A_0) 1_{\{(Q_0, A_0, I_0^u, \varphi_0) \in N^{S\mathcal{E}}\}} + \pi^R(Q_0, I_0^u, \varphi_0, A_0) 1_{\{(Q_0, A_0, I_0^u, \varphi_0) \in (N^{S\mathcal{E}})^c\}}$$

subject to,

$$A_0 \leq A^I \qquad\qquad \text{Dry Powder}$$

$$SQ_0 \leq \varphi_0 S^L Q_0 + I_0^u + A_0 \qquad \text{Budget}$$

$$I_0^u + \varphi_0 S^L Q_0 \leq \eta(SQ_0 + (A^I - A_0)) \qquad \text{Capital Requirement}$$

$$Q_0, I_0^u, A_0 \geq 0, \varphi_0 \in [0, \overline{\varphi}].$$

Conditional on being safe or risky, the firm is the residual claim from the initial portfolio, their private benefits, and the payoff from purchasing more of the asset in the refinancing period. The firm's restrictions are the same as in the stay regime: a dry powder bound, it's budget constraint, and it's capital requirements. Note that given firms' default costs, secured funding will be preferred over unsecured funding only if $S^L \geq \lambda C^L$. Otherwise the cost of raising secured funding would be too high and firms would only raise unsecured debt. Using the same parameter assumption as in the stay regime to ensure that firms that take on full leverage actually default, the solution to the firms initial financing problem in this regime is given by,

**Proposition 2.** *In the stay exemption regime if* $S > S^L$, $S^L \in (\lambda C^L, C^L]$ *and A1 holds, there exists a function* $b^{**}(S, S^L)$ *such that if* $b < b^{**}(S, S^L)$ *the solution to the firm's initial financing problem is*

$$Q_0^* = \begin{cases} 0 & \text{if } S > S^{BE}(S^L, b) \\ Q_0^{undet} & \text{if } S = S^{BE}(S^L, b) \\ \frac{A^I}{S - \eta S^L} & \text{if } S < S^{BE}(S^L, b), \end{cases}$$

*where* $Q_0^{undet}$ *may take any value between* $\left[0, \frac{A^I}{S^{BE}(S^L, b) - \eta S^L}\right]$ *and*

$$S^{BE}(S^L, b) = \frac{\overline{C} + b + (1 - \alpha)\left(\frac{C^L - S^L}{S^L(1-\eta)}\right)\eta S^L}{1 + (1-\alpha)\left(\frac{C^L - S^L}{S^L(1-\eta)}\right)}. \tag{7}$$

---

[28] In the interest of brevity, I shall omit the utility function's dependence on primitive parameters $A^I, b$, and the final period's price $S^L$.

If $b \geq b^{**}(S, S^L)$ the solution to the firm's initial financing problem is,

$$Q_0^* = \frac{A^I}{S(1 - \eta)}.$$

These strategies lead to the following payoffs,

$$\pi_0(S, S^L; b) = \begin{cases} (1 - \alpha)\left(\frac{C^L - S^L}{S^L(1 - \eta)}\right) A^I + A^I & \text{if } S \geq S^{BE}(S^L, b) \text{ and } b < b^{**}(S, S^L) \\ \frac{(\overline{C} + b - S)A^I}{S - \eta S^L} + A^I & \text{if } S < S^{BE}(S^L, b) \text{ and } b < b^{**}(S, S^L) \\ \frac{(C^D(\overline{\varphi}, S^L) + b - S)A^I}{S(1 - \eta)} + A^I & \text{if } b \geq b^{**}(S, S^L). \end{cases}$$

The solution to the firms' problem in this regime is similar to the solution in the previous one. Firms are either risky or safe, and if safe, their investment strategy depends on the breakeven price that induces them to participate. The important difference is that in this regime the safe firms' breakeven price (denoted by $S^{BE}(S^L, b)$) not only depends on firms' private benefits but also on the next period's market price, i.e., the fire sale. It can be easily verified that $S^{BE}(S^L, b)$ is increasing in $S^L$, which implies that a larger fire sale in the refinancing period increases firms' incentives not to participate in the initial market and hold on to their dry powder.

The intuition for this behavior is straight forward. If a safe firm invests in $t = 0$, it risks reducing its ability to purchase defaulted collateral at the fire sale price. Thus, it must be compensated to induce it to participate in the market initially, which translates into a lower breakeven price. It is important to note that if $S^L = C^L$, then $S^{BE}(S^L, b)$ is equal to $\overline{C} + b$. That is, absent the fire sale, safe firms' strategies and payoffs are exactly the same as in the stay regime.

With this in mind, whenever $b = 0$, $S^{BE}(S^L, 0)$ can be rearranged to give a more intuitive expression. After some algebraic manipulation $S^{BE}(S^L, 0)$ solves the following equality:

$$1 + \frac{(1 - \alpha)(C^L - S^L)}{S^L(1 - \eta)} = \frac{\overline{C}}{S} + \frac{(1 - \alpha)(C^L - S^L)}{S^L(1 - \eta)} \frac{\eta S^L}{S}, \tag{8}$$

for $S$. The left-hand side is the gross return of holding on to dry powder to purchase defaulted collateral at a fire sale price, and the right-hand side is the return from investing in the initial period. Dry powder receives a gross interest rate of 1 plus the expected net profit of $C^L - S^L$ of purchasing $1/(S^L(1 - \eta))$ of the defaulted collateral. The right-hand side gives a gross return of $\overline{C}/S$ plus the expected net profit of $C^L - S^L$ of purchasing $1/(S^L(1 - \eta))$ of the defaulted collateral. This last purchase is realized using $\eta S^L Q_0$ of the original asset as collateral, which has an initial costs $SQ_0$.[29] Thus, for a non private benefit firm to

---

[29] The size of the defaulted asset purchase can be appreciated in the expression of $Q_1^*$ in equation (6).

be indifferent between investing in $t = 0$ or $t = 1$, condition (8) must hold.

As in the stay regime, for high enough private benefits firms would be willing to assume the ex ante default costs. The equilibrium of interest will be one with parameter values such that private benefit firms will prefer to take on risky strategies, which will be the source of the asset supply in case of default. In the following section, conditions will be set so that in equilibrium private benefit firms choose a risky strategy over a safe one.

# 5    Equilibrium

This section analyzes the equilibrium outcome in both regimes. The main setting under consideration will have private benefit firms taking on risky positions in the first period and at least a fraction of non private benefit firms holding on to spare capacity for the second. These two conditions are necessary to have interesting equilibrium in the stay exemption regime: in $t = 1$ default is needed to generate a supply, and surviving firms need spare capacity to generate demand.

The initial risky asset supply $K$ is fixed and set exogenously. Firms' demand, the risky asset supply, and the fraction of private benefit firms $\theta$ pins down market clearing and the nature of the equilibrium. The relative size of the firm's initial endowment compared to the asset supply will be paramount to determine prices, especially to induce a fire sale in the stay exemption regime. The focus will be in a setting in which the stay regime's initial asset price is equal to its expected future cash flows. This is an economically reasonable starting point: With no forced sale in the refinancing period to cause a fire sale, demand and supply are such that prices reflect fundamental values. In the stay exemption regime, the same setting leads to a very different equilibrium outcome since the potential fire sale in the low state alters firms investment and financing decisions.

The equilibrium concept employed in the model is a standard Walrasian equilibrium. Specifically, given an initial endowment $A^I$, asset supply $K$, and a fraction $\theta$ of private benefit firms, an equilibrium is given by prices such that firms adopt optimal strategies and markets clear. The difference between regimes is that in the stay regime, firms' optimal strategies are characterized by Proposition 1 and market clearing is only imposed in $t = 0$. In the stay exemption, regime firms' initial strategies are given by Proposition 2 and market clearing is imposed in $t \in \{0, 1\}$.

## 5.1 Stay Regime

The equilibrium of interest for this regime has $S = \overline{C}$. If private benefit firms adopt a risky strategy, from Proposition 1 firms' individual demands are given by

$$Q_0^{PB} = \frac{A^I}{\overline{C}(1-\eta)}, \quad Q_0^{NPB} \in \left[0, \frac{A^I}{\overline{C} - \eta C^L}\right),$$

where $Q_0^{PB}$ and $Q_0^{NPB}$ denote private benefit and non private benefit firms' individual demand in $t = 0$. Given non private benefit firms indifference when $S = \overline{C}$ their individual demand cannot be precisely specified. But integrating over all agents and imposing market clearing, the resulting aggregate demand can be deduced. Thus, the initial fixed supply of the asset $K$ that results in an equilibrium with $S = \overline{C}$ is

$$K \in \left[\frac{A^I \theta}{\overline{C}(1-\eta)}, \frac{A^I \theta}{\overline{C}(1-\eta)} + \frac{A^I(1-\theta)}{\overline{C} - \eta C^L}\right) := [K_{min}, K_{max}^{\mathcal{S}}),$$

which corresponds to private benefit firms taking on risky strategies and $\overline{Q}_0^{NPB} \in \left[0, \frac{A^I(1-\theta)}{\overline{C} - \eta C^L}\right)$. In effect, for $K < K_{min}$ private benefit firms would still choose the maximum leverage allowed, increasing the asset price above $\overline{C}$. For $K > K_{max}^{\mathcal{S}}$, non private benefit firms would take on the maximum amount of leverage (though still avoiding default), reducing the asset price below $\overline{C}$.

To make sure private benefit firms adopt a risky strategy, the size of their position and magnitude of their benefits must compensate the cost of default. Specifically, from Proposition 1, private benefits must be set so that $b > b^*(\overline{C})$. This leads to the following theorem:

**Theorem 1.** *If parameter assumption A1 holds and $K \in [K_{min}, K_{max}^{\mathcal{S}})$, then there exists a $b^* > 0$ such that for all $b > b^*$ private benefit firms take on risky positions and non private benefit firms adopt safe strategies. In this setting, there exists a stay regime equilibrium with $S = \overline{C}$.*

Theorem 1 presents the benchmark setting from which to compare the outcomes of both regimes. The initial capital committed to the market $A^I$, the market composition $\theta$, and the supply of the asset $K$ are such that prices reflect fundamental values. Figure 3 shows non private benefit firms' individual demand and the resulting equilibrium in the stay regime. The following section will show that in the stay exemption regime prices deviate from fundamental values because capital must also be allocated to the refinancing period to purchase defaulted collateral.

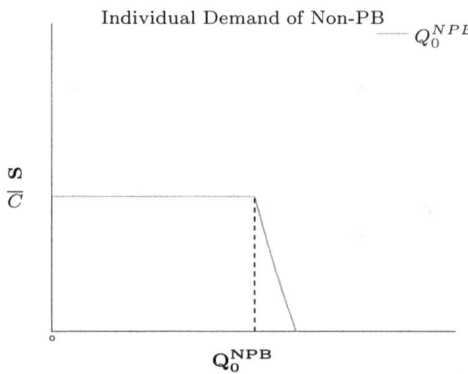
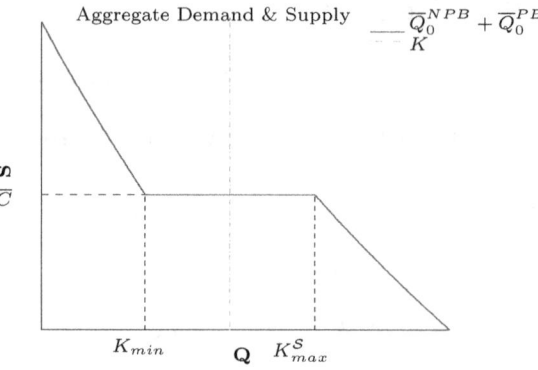

**Figure 3:** Stay Regime optimal strategies and equilibrium outcome — left hand side plot show the individual demand of a non private benefit firm in the stay regime when $S = \overline{C}$. Right hand side shows firms aggregate demand, and the relevant range where the asset supply implies prices equal to fundamental value. $A^I = 1, C^H = 110, C^L = 70, \alpha = .9, \lambda = .5, \eta = .75, \varphi = .5$.

## 5.2 Stay Exemption Regime

In this regime, market clearing is imposed in both the initial and refinancing period. In the refinancing period, the supply of defaulted assets comes from secured lenders who received collateral from bankrupt firms and demand stems from solvent firms raising additional funds to purchase those assets.

The special feature of this regime is the possibility of a fire sale, which creates a premium for having spare capacity in period $t = 1$. When firms decide not to exhaust their debt capacity in $t = 0$ they have the potential to purchase the asset at a discounted price in period $t = 1$, increasing their expected profits. This premium for liquidity creates a reduction in the breakeven price for non private benefit firms to participate in the market initially: firms must be compensated in the initial period to give up the additional upside of holding on to dry powder.

Depending on the severity of the subsequent fire sale, the price discount in period $t = 0$ could also induce a group of non private benefit firms to take on risky positions initially. That is, the initial price discount could be large enough to compensate non private benefit firms to bear the cost of a potential default. This would give rise to an equilibrium where a fraction of non private benefit firms adopt a safe strategy and the remainder take a risky one. Considering the payoff functions characterized in Proposition 2, the indifference condition $\pi_0^S(S, S^L; 0) = \pi_0^R(S, S^L; 0)$ is equivalent to[30]

$$1 + (1 - \alpha)\frac{C^L - S^L}{S^L(1 - \eta)} = 1 + \frac{C^D(\overline{\varphi}, S^L) - S}{S(1 - \eta)}. \tag{9}$$

The left-hand side of condition (9) is the gross expected return of holding on to dry powder to purchase the defaulted asset at a fire price. The right-hand side is the expected return from taking on a levered

---

[30]In terms of Proposition 2 this occurs whenever $b^{**}(S, S^L) = 0$.

position that results in default if the asset has a bad outcome. The additional leverage stemming from a depressed price is enough to compensate the loss from default and the missed opportunity of earning a fire sale profit. The asset price that satisfies this condition will be denoted $S^M$: if $S > S^M$ non private benefit firms will only undertake safe strategies; if $S = S^M(S^L)$ there will be mixing where a fraction $\xi$ of these firms will take a risky strategy.

Under the assumption that private benefits are high enough for those firms to adopt a risky strategy in the initial period, Proposition 2 characterizes their individual demand in $t = 0$. Integrating over all private benefit firms, their aggregate demand in the first and second period is

$$\overline{Q}_0^{PB} = \frac{A^I \theta}{S(1 - \eta)}, \quad \overline{Q}_1^{PB} = -\frac{\overline{\varphi} A^I \theta}{S(1 - \eta)}, \tag{10}$$

where the negative sign in $\overline{Q}_1^{PB}$ indicates these firms are supplying the asset in the second period. Note that only $\overline{\varphi}$ of private benefit firms' risky asset position is supplied in $t = 1$, i.e., the fraction earmarked to secured lenders.

Conditional on $S$, non private benefit firms have three potential strategies they could undertake in $t = 0$. They could take a relatively small position leaving some debt capacity for the refinancing period, adopt a fully levered position risking default in the down state, or refrain from investing altogether to take advantage of the fire sale. These strategies, characterized by Proposition 2, lead to four potential aggregate strategies:

1. **Dry Powder Strategy (DP):** Non private benefit firms hold on to dry powder for the next period,

$$\overline{Q}_0^{NPB} = 0, \quad \overline{Q}_1^{NPB} = \frac{A^I(1 - \theta)}{S^L(1 - \eta)}, \tag{11}$$

which occurs whenever $S > S^{BE}(S^L; 0)$ and $S > S^M(S^L)$.

2. **Breakeven Strategy (BE):** Non private benefit firms participate in the initial asset purchase but maintain spare capacity to purchase the defaulted asset in $t = 1$,

$$\overline{Q}_0^{NPB} = \overline{Q}_0^{undet} \in \left[0, \frac{A^I(1 - \theta)}{S - \eta S^L}\right), \quad \overline{Q}_1^{NPB} = \frac{A^I(1 - \theta) - (S - \eta S^L)\overline{Q}_0^{NPB}}{S^L(1 - \eta)}, \tag{12}$$

which occurs whenever $S = S^{BE}(S^L; 0)$ and $S > S^M(S^L)$.

3. **Dry Powder Mixing Strategy (DPmix):** A fraction $\xi$ of non private benefit firms take on risky positions and the remaining hold on to dry powder for the following period,

$$\overline{Q}_0^{NPB} = \frac{A^I(1 - \theta)\xi}{S(1 - \eta)}, \quad \overline{Q}_1^{NPB} = \frac{A^I(1 - \theta)(1 - \xi)}{S^L(1 - \eta)} - \frac{\varphi A^I(1 - \theta)\xi}{S(1 - \eta)}, \tag{13}$$

which occurs whenever $S > S^{BE}(S^L; 0)$ and $S = S^M(S^L)$.

4. **Breakeven Mixing Strategy (BEmix):** A fraction $\xi$ of non private benefit firms take on risky positions and the remaining participate in the initial asset purchase but maintain spare capacity to purchase the defaulted asset in $t = 1$,

$$\overline{Q}_0^{NPB} = \overline{Q}_0^{undet} + \frac{A^I(1-\theta)\xi}{S(1-\eta)} \quad \text{with} \quad \overline{Q}_0^{undet} \in \left[0, \frac{A^I(1-\theta)(1-\xi)}{S-\eta S^L}\right), \tag{14}$$

$$\overline{Q}_1^{NPB} = \frac{A^I(1-\theta)(1-\xi) - (S-\eta S^L)\overline{Q}_0^{undet}}{S^L(1-\eta)} - \frac{\varphi A^I(1-\theta)\xi}{S(1-\eta)}, \tag{15}$$

which occurs whenever $S = S^{BE}(S^L; 0)$ and $S = S^M(S^L)$.

### 5.2.1   Dry Powder - Dry Powder Mixing Strategy

This subsection focuses on a parameterization that gives rise to a simple and tractable equilibrium outcome: Non private benefit firms either adopt a Dry Powder or a Dry Powder Mixing strategy. This approach simplifies the analysis since in both cases it isn't necessary to characterize non private benefit firms' safe demand in $t = 0$. The main conclusions of the model will be illustrated for these specific equilibrium outcomes, but the results will not depend on the parameter assumptions adopted herein.

To compare the equilibrium of this regime to the benchmark case characterized in Theorem 1 where asset prices reflect fundamental values, I assume $K \in [K_{min}, K_{max}^{\mathcal{S}})$. The main difference between regimes characterized in this paper stems from an environment where the potential shortage of capital in $t = 1$ induces a fire sale in the down state. To that effect, the fraction of private benefit firms is set so that solvent firms' demand isn't sufficient for prices to reflect fundamental values. Therefore, $\theta$ is set so that the split between private benefit and non private benefit firms implies $S = \overline{C}$ and $S^L = C^L$ when $K = K_{min}$. In other words, for the minimum asset supply, all non private benefit firms adopt a dry powder strategy, and their demand is high enough for prices to reflect fundamental values in the down state. Arguably, this is a rather extreme case, since any increase in asset supply will entail a shortage of capital in the refinancing period, yet it is useful to illustrate the model's main result. Accordingly, parameter assumptions are specified as follows:

**Assumption A2.** *The fraction of private benefit firms $\theta$ is such that non private benefit firms take a DP strategy for $K = K_{min}$, and market clearing prices are $S = \overline{C}$ and $S^L = C^L$: $\theta = \frac{\overline{C}}{\overline{C} + \overline{\varphi} C^L}$.*

To ensure that non private benefit firms don't choose to participate safely in $t = 0$ (which is only assumed for tractability), parameters must be set so that $S > S^{BE}(S^L, 0)$,

**Assumption A3.** *Non private benefit firms do not take a BE strategy:* $S > S^{BE}(S^L, 0)$: $\frac{\overline{C}}{C^L} > \frac{(1-\alpha)\eta}{\eta - \alpha}$.

Conditions must also be provided so that private benefit firms do in fact choose a risky strategy in $t = 0$. This is guaranteed if $b > b^{**}(S, S^L)$ of Proposition 2 for all $(S, S^L)$ in equilibrium. In addition, to use Proposition 2 directly the fire sale price must be larger than the default value of the asset: $S^L > \lambda C^L$. This condition incentivizes risky firms to exhaust their secured funding first, which should hold for the lowest fire sale price,

**Assumption A4.** *The fire sale price is larger than the default value of the asset* $S^L > \lambda C^L$ *for all* $K \in [K_{min}, K_{max}^{\mathcal{S}}]$: $\frac{\overline{C}}{C^L} > \eta + \frac{\lambda(1-\eta)\overline{\varphi}}{1-\lambda}$.

Finally, the interest of this subsection is to consider a setting in which the initial discount is large enough to induce a fraction of non private benefit firms to take on risky positions: $S = S^M$. That is, the mismatch between private benefit firm demand and asset supply is large enough to motivate more risk taking,

**Assumption A5.** *The initial asset price $S$ is equal to $S^M$ for some* $K^M \in [K_{min}, K_{max}^{\mathcal{S}}]$: $\frac{(1-\overline{\varphi})(1-\lambda)}{\alpha \overline{C} - (1-\alpha)[\overline{\varphi} + (1-\overline{\varphi})(1-\lambda)]C^L} < \frac{\overline{\varphi}(1-\eta)}{\overline{C} - \eta C^L}$.

All of the aforementioned assumptions put together lead to the following result,

**Theorem 2.** *If parameter assumptions A1 – A5 hold then there exists $b^{**} > 0$, $K^M$, and $K_{max}^{\mathcal{SE}} \leq K_{max}^{\mathcal{S}}$ such that for all $b > b^{**}$ private benefit firms take on risky strategies. For $K \in [K_{min}, K^M]$ non private benefit firms adopt a DP strategy, and for $K \in (K^M, K_{max}^{\mathcal{SE}})$ non private benefit firms adopt a DPmix strategy. In this setting, for $K \in [K_{min}, K^M]$, there exists a stay exemption regime equilibrium with*

$$
\begin{aligned}
S &= \frac{A^I \theta}{K(1-\eta)}, \\
S^L &= \frac{1-\theta}{\overline{\varphi}\theta} S.
\end{aligned}
$$

*For $K \in (K^M, K_{max}^{\mathcal{SE}})$, there exists a stay exemption regime equilibrium with*

$$
\begin{aligned}
S &= \frac{A^I(\theta + \xi(1-\theta))}{K(1-\eta)}, \\
S^L &= \frac{(1-\theta)(1-\xi)}{\overline{\varphi}(\theta + \xi(1-\theta))} S, \\
(1-\alpha)\left(\frac{C^L}{S^L} - 1\right) &= \frac{C^D(\overline{\varphi}, S^L)}{S} - 1,
\end{aligned}
$$

*where $\xi > 0$ is the fraction of private benefit firms that take on risky strategies.*

23

The equilibrium characterized in Theorem 2 has non private benefit firms take a dry powder strategy whenever $K$ is low and a dry powder mixing strategy when $K$ is high. This equilibrium outcome highlights one of the main results of the paper: The stay exemption can induce more firms to adopt risky strategies.

### 5.2.2 Breakeven – Breakeven Mixing Strategy: Numerical Exercise

It can be shown that similar conclusions result from alternative setups with different equilibrium outcomes. Many of the previously parameter assumptions can be dismissed, which were only adopted for tractability; but others are important for fire sales to manifest themselves and for additional risk-taking to arise. In particular, it is necessary to have a shortage of capital in the refinancing period, which was adopted by Assumption A2. Maintaining this assumption, and ensuring that private benefit firms prefer levered strategies in $t = 0$ (i.e., a high enough $b$), Figure 4 shows the resulting first-period price, fire sale price, and fraction of non private benefit firms that adopt a risky strategy.

For relatively low levels of asset supply, non private benefit firms invest some of their capital initially, holding spare capacity for the fire sale. For higher levels of $K$, non private benefit firms reduce their purchase in $t = 0$, which is picked up by firms that take on risky strategies. Finally, for relatively large values of $K$, non private benefit firms either wait for the fire sale or take on a risky position initially.

## 5.3   Comparative Statics

This subsection explores how the equilibrium of both regimes react differently to changes in underlying parameters. The main variables of interest are firms capital requirement $\eta$, which effectively caps surviving firms demand in the stay exemption regime resulting in a fire sale; the firms value upon default $\lambda$, which measures the economic loss of a firm's default; and changes in the probability of of a good outcome $\alpha$.

Changes in the stay regime equilibrium are relatively straight forward. Private benefit firms' portfolios remain largely unchanged: They take out the maximum amount of leverage allowed. Non private benefit firm aggregate demand increases or decreases, adjusting to different supply levels to maintain prices at fundamental values. Therefore, the equilibrium price remains the same for changes in $\lambda$ and $\eta$, and changes in $\alpha$ are straight forward.

The more interesting exercise is to study how parameter changes can alter the stay exemption regime equilibrium. The analytical characterization of Theorem 2 and Lemma 1 in the appendix, shows that when

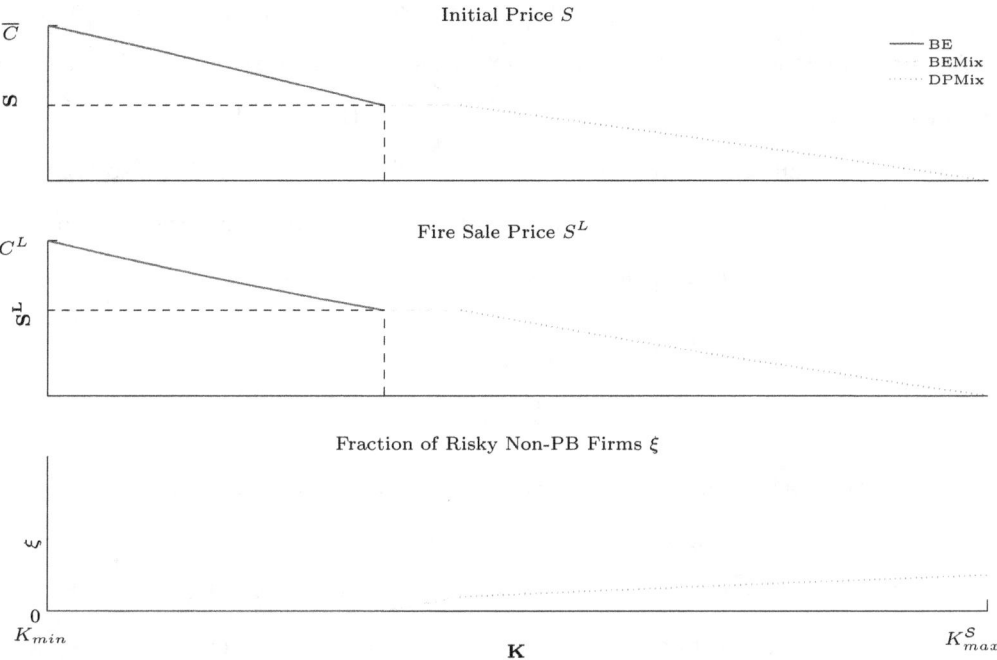

**Figure 4:** Breakeven, Breakeven Mixing, and Dry Powder Mixing Strategy equilibrium outcomes — plot shows the initial price, the fire sale price, and the fraction of firms that adopt risky strategies in period $t = 0$. For low levels of asset supply non private benefit firms take a breakeven strategy. Higher levels of supply depress the initial price until some non private benefit firms mix between risky and safe strategies. For relatively high levels of asset supply, non private benefit firms cease to participate safely in the initial market. Parameter values are: $A^I = 1, C^H = 110, C^L = 70, \alpha = .9, \lambda = .5, \eta = .75,$ and $\varphi = .5$

non private benefit firms take a dry powder strategy the equilibrium changes as follows:

$$\frac{\partial S}{\partial \eta} > 0 \quad \frac{\partial S}{\partial \lambda} = 0 \quad \frac{\partial S}{\partial \alpha} = 0.$$

As capital requirements increase, firms' ability to take on leverage is greater. This generates higher levels of demand in the initial financing period, increasing the $S$. The effect on $S^L$ is only transmitted through changes in $S$. Though higher leverage in the initial period increases the supply of defaulted collateral in $t = 1$, solvent firms have larger purchasing power in the down state, canceling the effect. Thus, the only real effect is in the initial price increase. In this equilibrium, changes in $\lambda$ and $\alpha$ don't have an impact on prices since firms' decisions remain the same: Private benefit firms still insist on taking a risky position initially, and non private benefit firms still opt to hold their dry powder for the second.

The analysis when the equilibrium outcome involves non private benefit mixing into risky strategies is slightly more involved. Using the characterization of Theorem 2, and adopting the additional parameter assumption of $\theta > (1 - \alpha)$, Lemma 1 in the appendix gives the following result:[31]

$$\frac{\partial S}{\partial \eta} > 0 \quad \frac{\partial S}{\partial \lambda} > 0 \quad \frac{\partial S}{\partial \alpha} > 0,$$
$$\frac{\partial \xi}{\partial \eta} < 0 \quad \frac{\partial \xi}{\partial \lambda} > 0 \quad \frac{\partial \xi}{\partial \alpha} > 0.$$

Changes in $\eta$ cause the initial asset price to increase, since private benefit firms are able to increase their position, pushing up the price. The impact on $\xi$ stems from the increase in $S$, which reduces non private benefit firms profits for taking risky strategies. The increase in $\lambda$ is straight forward: a higher value for defaulted assets reduces financing costs for firms who take risky strategies. This increases the fraction of non private benefit firms who participate in the initial asset purchase and therefore increases the initial asset price. An increase in $\alpha$ implies an increase in profits for a risky strategy and a decrease in profits in a dry powder strategy, and the fraction of non private benefit firms who adopt risky strategies increases, raising the market clearing price. The effects on the fire sale price can be deduced from the interaction between $S$ and $\xi$. Lemma 1 states

$$\frac{\partial S^L}{\partial \eta} > 0 \quad \frac{\partial S^L}{\partial \lambda} < 0 \quad \frac{\partial S^L}{\partial \alpha} < 0.$$

As $\lambda$ and $\alpha$ increase, the payoff for undertaking risky strategies also increase, therefore more non private benefit capital migrates to the first period, increasing the fire sale (i.e., reducing $S^L$). Increases in $\eta$ result in an increase in the initial asset price and a reduction in the non private benefit firms who take risky strategies, which increases $S^L$.

---

[31]Note that in the appendix $p = \theta + \xi(1 - \theta)$, and $\frac{\partial \xi}{\partial x} = \frac{\partial p}{\partial x} \frac{1}{(1-\theta)}$.

# 6 Model Discussion

In this section I discuss the main trade-offs in the stay vs. stay exemption debate for repos and highlight in which market the potential of a fire sale is likely to be a first-order effect relative to other aspects. Specifically, I argue that a fire sale of repo collateral is more relevant for illiquid markets that may suffer from cash-in-the-market pricing and for assets that do not have any additional benefits beyond their pay off. In addition, I will provide anecdotal evidence of the model's main mechanism, namely firms' incentive to hold on to dry powder to exploit future fire sales.

## 6.1 Stay vs. Stay Exemption Discussion

In the context of repo, the potential benefits of automatic stay exemption can be summarized as follows: a reduction in creditors' incentives to run and the liberation of collateral that can be used more efficiently elsewhere.[32] With regard to the first point, Skeel and Jackson (2012) provide anecdotal evidence that the stay exemption had little or no effect on lenders' incentives to renew their loans with debtors that were perceived to be in financial trouble. Even though creditors were certain to receive the underlying collateral in case of a firm bankruptcy, they preferred to avoid a default event altogether. This preference casts doubt on the effectiveness of repo's exemption from stay to mitigate runs on a firm.

The liberation of assets tied up in a bankruptcy proceeding may be a compelling argument if the assets in question have additional benefits above and beyond their payoff. In effect, U.S. Treasury securities do provide added value given their flexibility to use as collateral to raise funding and their relatively low risk, which helps firms fulfill regulatory capital requirements. These additional benefits have been documented for on-the-run Treasuries, measured by the difference between the general collateral repo rate and the repo rate on a specific instrument, which is referred to as an asset's *specialness* (see Duffie (1996)). For these types of assets the effective "lock-up" of collateral could limit the additional benefits they may bring. But this issue may not be as relevant for assets in a relatively thin and illiquid market. In fact, during the financial crisis it was precisely the use of MBS as collateral that created difficulties for firms to raise funding (see Krishnamurthy et al. (2012) for evidence of the contraction of repo's using MBS). Thus, the efficient use of collateral is not likely to be an important factor for the types of markets this paper has in mind.

Key potential costs in the stay vs. stay exemption debate relevant for repos are: counterparties limited incentive to monitor, firm's inefficient substitution from traditional financing, and the potential to trigger a fire sale.[33] The first point, stressed by Roe (2011), may have limited importance in the context of money

---

[32]A detailed analysis of the key arguments surrounding the stay vs. stay exemption debate, along with their intuition, is given by Duffie and Skeel (2012).

[33]Another potential cost is firms' reduced incentives to file for bankruptcy, given that exemptions from stay limit bankruptcy

market funds financing large broker–dealers whose operational complexities would be hard to gauge from an outsider's perspective. With regard to a firm's preferred financing vehicle, though it is true that repo's exemption from stay makes it less costly, an additional friction must be taken into account to argue a reduction in the firms total financing cost. Moreover, why would an increase in repo funding relative to other alternatives be "inefficient"? The default costs in this paper do give firms incentives to increase their repo funding, which is beneficial since only non-earmarked assets suffer a default cost. But these features of the model are assumed. To address this issue a more extensive analysis is necessary taking into account firms' total debt capacity, incorporating a specific friction to explain firms' preference for repo funding, and specifying the inefficiency stemming from the excessive use of repo. Although this may be an interesting analysis, it is outside the scope of this paper.

Given the above, a fire sale stemming from the mass sale of collateral posted by defaulted firms is arguably an important aspect in the debate for relatively illiquid markets.[34] The model in this paper not only addresses the consequences during the fire sale, but also studies the effects on markets before the default event. The partial evidence provided in subsection 6.2 suggests that the mechanism of hoarding liquidity and its impact on prices could have played an important role in the MBS market during the 2007–2009 financial crisis.

## 6.2 Supporting Evidence

The model presented in this paper points to a liquidity hoarding mechanism that ultimately results in an ex ante price reduction that alters firms' decisions. In essence, the main difference between regimes is that the stay exemption regime increases firms' investment opportunity set, attracting capital to exploit a future fire sale and causing the initial price to deviate from fundamentals.

In a related paper, Acharya et al. (2011) provide anecdotal evidence of instances when firms strategically hoarded liquidity to take advantage of future price dislocations. They present the case of National City Bank, which later became Citibank, that foresaw the banking panic of 1893 and 1907 and strategically accumulated liquidity to take advantage of the future crisis. In both cases, before the crisis National City Bank accumulated significantly larger reserve ratios than other competing banks. This allowed the firm to increase deposits and expand their lending while other competitors were forced to contract. The motivation behind the bank's strategic decision was made evident by a quote from the bank's president prior to the 1907 crisis, "If by able and judicious management we have money to help our dealers when trust companies

---

protection. But in the context of repo financing this is related to the potential withdrawal of funds from creditors – that is, a run.

[34]Fire sales were a prime concern for regulators in the 2007–09 financial crisis. See Skeel and Jackson (2012) for details.

have suspended, we will have all the business we want for many years."[35]

Acharya et al. (2011) also provide anecdotal evidence of communications with bankers during the recent financial crisis, who claimed that the "...reasons for drying up of inter-bank lending markets has been the hoarding of liquidity by banks for acquisitions of troubled institutions at fire-sale prices, the other two reasons being precautionary motive from the risk of being distressed oneself and adverse selection about borrowing institutions." This suggests that during the crisis firms may have had the capacity to purchase assets, but refrained from doing so to await the collapse of another firm that would trigger a fire sale.

One interpretation of the model in the context of the financial crisis of 2007–09 is to consider private benefit firms as dealer banks and hedge funds holding large positions of MBS. Krishnamurthy et al. (2012) show that before the demise of Bear Stearns, 50% of repo transactions of four important dealer banks used non-agency MBS as underlying collateral (see Figure 8 of that paper). Table 7 in He et al. (2010) provides evidence that these same firms had substantial positions in credit and mortgage-related securities before the crisis. Non private benefit firms can be thought of as commercial banks who also had significant positions in MBS, but didn't rely as heavily on repo to finance them (see Gorton and Metrick (2012) pp. 443). Arguably, the total leverage of dealer banks and hedge funds was larger than that of the commercial banking sector, which at that time had considerably more regulatory restrictions. Evidence from the financial crisis suggests that the banking sector as a whole did have liquidity, yet opted not to use it. He et al. (2010) provide evidence of a mass sale of securitized products by hedge funds and dealer banks (approximately $800 billion), much of which was picked up by commercial banks (approximately $550 billion). But on aggregate the commercial banking sector actually increased its liquidity holdings, with support from the government, which highlights the sector's limited participation in MBS.

Although the above analysis is subject to different interpretations, these stylized facts fit well with the arguments presented in this paper. The fact that commercial banks, which possessed the expertise to participate in the MBS market, held back some of their cash points to the mechanism of the model. As was previously mentioned, this could have been for precautionary reasons or a potential lemons problem in the market, but this behavior is also consistent with liquidity hoarding. The lack of demand for these assets in expectation of other firms defaulting, triggering a fire sale, could well have affected pricing throughout the crisis.

---

[35]For more details of the case, see Cleveland et al. (1985).

# 7 Equilibrium Analysis and Extensions

This section presents a cost–benefit analysis of the equilibrium under both regimes, some potential policy implications, and alternative settings of the model. Specifically, the policy subsection will consider alternatives in the stay exemption regime that would mitigate any distortions stemming from a fire sale. The model extension considers a setting where neither firms nor lenders internalize the potential fire sale, aggravating the price discount in a default event.

## 7.1 Cost–Benefit Analysis

The main distortions in the model are firms' private benefits for holding large risky asset positions[36] vs. the deadweight cost brought on by default. These are the distortions that induce firms to take on leverage or refrain from doing so. Though it may be misleading to talk of "welfare" in such a stylized setting,[37] one can at least weigh the positive and negative aspects within the model.

Private benefits are proportional to the size of the risky asset position held by private benefit firms in $t = 0$, and the deadweight costs are the losses incurred by all defaulting firms. Therefore, the expected benefits and costs are

$$\text{PB gain} = b\frac{\theta A^I}{S(1 - \eta)}, \tag{16}$$

$$\text{Total Cost} = (1 - \overline{\varphi})(1 - \lambda)(1 - \alpha)C^L\frac{(\theta + (1 - \theta)\xi)A^I}{S(1 - \eta)}, \tag{17}$$

where a fraction $\xi \geq 0$ of non private benefit firms take risky strategies. Note that the costs $(1 - \lambda$ of the expected portfolio value in the down state) are assumed by all firms that take risky strategies, which affects the non-earmarked fraction $(1 - \overline{\varphi})$ of their portfolio. From these expressions it is clear that whenever $\xi > 0$ costs are proportionally larger than benefits, since private benefits are only perceived by a fixed fraction of firms, whereas costs are borne by all firms who choose a risky strategy.

In the stay regime, from Theorem 1, the economy's costs and benefits do not depend on $K \in [K_{min}, K_{max}^S)$. In effect,

$$\text{PB gain} = bK_{min}, \quad \text{Total Cost} = (1 - \overline{\varphi})(1 - \lambda)(1 - \alpha)C^L K_{min}.$$

Since the fraction of firms that undertake risky strategies remains the same and prices are fixed for all $K \in [K_{min}, K_{max}^S)$, firms' portfolios remain unchanged, making costs and benefits constant. In effect, in

---

[36] It is important not to misinterpret the labeling of the model's "benefits". These benefits are only perceived by firms that take on large amounts of debt, and in fact are just a modeling device to alter these agents' incentives. They should be thought of as firms' *incentive distortion*, rather than benefits for the economy.

[37] For example, it would be necessary to incorporate the impact on agents supplying the asset initially, which is outside the scope of this paper.

this regime the same amount of the asset supply is held by private benefit firms, which are the only firms that risk default.[38]

This is not the the case in the stay exemption regime. In a setting where Theorem 2 holds for $K \in [K_{min}^{\mathcal{S}}, K^M]$ (when $\xi = 0$), replacing the initial market clearing price in equation (16) and (17) gives

$$\text{PB gain} = bK, \quad \text{Total Cost} = (1 - \overline{\varphi})(1 - \lambda)(1 - \alpha)C^L K.$$

As in the stay regime, the ex ante costs and benefits are borne by private benefit firms. But since they are the only type of firm participating in the market initially, their risky asset position becomes larger for higher levels of asset supply. Thus, they enjoy more benefits but also pay for more costly default. When the equilibrium outcome has a fraction $\xi$ of non private benefit firms mixing, from Theorem 2 when $K \in (K^M, K_{max}^{\mathcal{SE}})$, the private benefits and costs are

$$\text{PB gain} = \frac{\theta}{\theta + \xi(1 - \theta)}bK, \quad \text{Total Cost} = (1 - \overline{\varphi})(1 - \lambda)(1 - \alpha)C^L K.$$

The cost–benefit analysis for this equilibrium outcome is similar to the previous one: The initial asset supply is purchased by firms who adopt risky strategies — either private benefit or non private benefit firms. Note that in this case the total cost has the same expression as when $K \in [K_{min}^{\mathcal{S}}, K^M]$, but the benefits are only reaped by a fraction of those firms that risk default. Therefore, this outcome has proportionally more costs than benefits because of mixing.

In case the equilibrium outcome consisted of non private benefit firms participating safely in the initial asset purchase (i.e., a breakeven or breakeven mixing strategy), the results would be qualitatively the same. In this scenario, for higher levels of $K$ there would be a price depreciation, increasing private benefit firms' asset position and giving rise to higher private benefits and higher default costs. No matter what the equilibrium outcome in the stay exemption regime, the costs and benefits increase as cash-in-the-market pricing deviates prices from fundamentals. Whereas in the stay regime, since prices reflect fundamental values, private benefit firms' participation is constant, thus the costs and benefits are held at a minimum.

---

[38]Note that if there were an additional cost for locking up secured asset in the stay regime, the total costs would take on the following form: $[\overline{\varphi}(1 - \hat{\lambda}) + (1 - \overline{\varphi})(1 - \lambda)](1 - \alpha)C^L K_{min}$ where $\hat{\lambda}$ (with $\hat{\lambda} < \lambda$ to ensure a preference for secured loans) would be the distress cost of resolving secured collateral in bankruptcy. Then the comparison between regimes would involve comparing this expression with the cost under stay exemption, which implies a condition between exogenous parameters. To keep the analysis simple, I have assumed secured lending is always resolved seamlessly.

## 7.2 Policy Recommendations

The motivation of this paper is to ask which regime is best when firms face a potential fire sale in the future. The analysis in subsection 7.1 shows that in the stay regime costs and benefits (i.e., incentive distortions) are held at a minimum, whereas in the stay exemption regime these trade offs will vary with the ratio of asset supply to initial capital committed to the market. Therefore, a reasonable policy implication may be to maintain these distortions and costs to a minimum, which is equivalent to eliminating any cash-in-the-market effects that cause prices to deviate from fundamentals. At the very least, this would deter non private benefit firms from undertaking risky strategies, unduly increasing the amount of default in the economy. From that perspective, the policy recommendation would be to have repo subject to automatic stays; at least for the type of collateral this paper has in mind. But there may be other reasons to want repo exempt from automatic stay that are not captured in this model, prompting other solutions to the cash-in-the-market distortion. I consider two possibilities: an intervention by the government and a contract modification to eliminate incentives to sell after default.

### 7.2.1 Government Asset Purchase

If a large outside investor without capital constraints were to commit to purchase defaulted assets in case of a bad outcome, the fire sale would completely disappear along with any distortions it causes. The natural agent to undertake this task would be the government. In this context, agents would internalize that in the refinancing period the market clearing condition would take on the following form:

$$\overline{Q}_1^{PB} + \overline{Q}_1^{NPB} + G = 0,$$

where $G$ would be the government's demand for defaulted collateral. The role of the government would be to purchase the asset until $S^L = C^L$, eliminating any ex ante fire sale premium. Thus, non private benefit firm capital can be totally committed in the initial financing period (i.e, $\overline{Q}_1^{NPB} = 0$), essentially reducing the setup to the stay regime.

Though this is a relatively simple exercise in the context of the model, this may not be as straightforward in practice. Besides a commitment by the government to purchase assets in case of a cash-in-the-market discount, the government must be able to recognize whether a price reduction is in fact due to limited liquidity or a deterioration in fundamentals. This evaluation would be difficult to do at a moment's notice. Moreover, the government's strategy does involve some degree of risk since $C^L > C^{LL}$, which may be undesirable. In spite of that, efforts made by the government during the 2007–09 financial crisis can be interpreted as exactly that: an attempt to purchase assets trading at prices below their economic value.

### 7.2.2 Lender Participation and Contracting Change

An important ingredient of the model is lenders' incentives to sell the asset upon default, irrespective of its trading price. This is motivated by two aspects that can be observed in current market practice. First, many of the lenders participating in repos have restrictions on holding risky long-dated assets. In addition, given the specific contracting arrangement of repos, conditional on wanting to sell the lender has limited interest in the final price. This is because any upside on the collateral after the loan is repaid is property of the original borrower. In the model, this is taken to an extreme since the initial face value on the loan is set to the fire sale price, eliminating all incentives to hold the asset.

In a world in which the lender does in fact receive the asset's upside after default, risk-neutral lenders that have the ability to hold the asset would have no incentive to sell it in the presence of a fire sale. In essence, the return that was previously captured by solvent firms that purchased the defaulted collateral would now disappear. These changes would imply that trade only occurs whenever $S^L = C^L$, irrespective of the amount of capital held by firms. By eliminating the fire sale, there is no initial price discount and the resulting equilibrium is identical to the stay regime.

In the context of the model, this modification must be considered carefully. An important ingredient of the paper is market segmentation and limited capital committed to the market. Specifically, the standing assumption throughout the model is that lenders cannot participate in the risky asset market directly. This is motivated by some expertise necessary to actively trade in the market that firms are initially endowed with. Allowing lenders to hold on to their collateral in case of default, effectively participating in the market in the down state, leads to the question, why didn't they participate initially? It could be argued that the initial asset purchase still involves some degree of expertise because of an unmodeled lemons problem present in the risky asset market, with which lenders need not concern themselves once they receive collateral from a defaulted firm. From this perspective the "bad" assets were already filtered out by expert firms in the initial stage.

An important aspect of this policy prescription is that it does not rely on an active government. In this setting, firms and lenders would eliminate the potential fire sale themselves. Undoubtedly, this recommendation would have important effects on other aspects of the repo market, particularly in the determination of haircuts. But for the analysis of this paper, the outcome is straightforward.

## 7.3 Myopic Agents

An interesting exercise is to consider a case in which agents in the economy do not internalize the potential fire sale that can arise in the stay exemption regime. Specifically, firms and lenders do not realize that, because of limited capital in the down state, the market clearing price may be below the asset's expected future payoff, perhaps because the total initial capital committed to the market is believed to be sufficient to satisfy any supply shock. This outcome results in non private benefit firms committing their capital in the first period, disregarding the potential payoff from a future fire sale. In the very least, this implies less capital in the refinancing state and a more severe fire sale.

More formally, in the stay exemption regime, non private benefit firms would adopt the strategy characterized by Proposition 2 where $S^L = C^L$. In this case, the breakeven price is equal to the fundamental value of the asset: $S^{BE}(C^L, 0) = \overline{C}$. Therefore, for $K \in [K_{min}, K^S_{max})$ non private benefit firms would increase aggregate demand until the first-period price equals the asset's fundamental value. Given the linear structure of the problem whenever the trading price equals the breakeven price, non private benefit firms' individual demand is undetermined. Thus, for a given asset supply $K$, it is unclear how many non private benefit firms would have raised debt to cause them to default. This implies that in the down state aggregate demand and supply is undetermined since it cannot be established how many firms will default nor how much spare capacity surviving firms will have. What is clear is that surviving firms' aggregate demand in $t = 1$ will be lower compared to a setting where agents account for the fire sale, making the price distortion even larger. This larger price distortion is because there is less dry powder to raise funds in the refinancing period and because the fire sale will reduce firm debt capacity substantially.

This setting arises naturally in instances where there is uncertainty as to the severity of any cash-in-the-market pricing. During March 2008, because of Bear Stearn's financial troubles, regulators "...worried that a mass sale of repo collateral could drive down the values of mortgage-related securities and further destabilize the markets."[39] In the myopic model, because of repos' exemption from stay and the degree of uncertainty around the amount of capital available to withstand a supply shock, the magnitude of the fire sale would be impossible to determine. Moreover, the severity of the fire sale could cause woes for other firms, exacerbating the illiquidity problem further by triggering more defaults. This is precisely the type of externality policy makers are currently concerned with when considering fire sales in repo markets (see Stein (2013)).

## 8 Concluding Remarks

This paper explores the consequences of repo's exemption from automatic stay in the presence of potential fire sales that result from limited capital committed to a market. The main finding of the paper is that future fire sales alter firms investment opportunity set, giving them incentives to hold their initial capital to take

---

[39]See Skeel and Jackson (2012).

advantage of a possible price discount in the future. This implies that more of the risky asset is held by firms that have incentives to take on high levels of leverage, increasing the amount assets held by defaulting firms, which is assumed to be costly. The mechanism disappears when repo is subject to stay, since in the model secured lenders receive their payments when market turmoil has subsided and prices reflect fundamental values.

A mix of ingredients is necessary for fire sales to arise endogenously in the model. The firms that participate in the risky asset market must have limited resources. Though they receive funding from an unconstrained lending sector, they have a ceiling on the amount of funding they can raise because of regulatory or skin-in-the-game constraints. These funding constraints limit the size of their risky asset position, which induces cash-in-the-market pricing. Importantly a fraction of firms have incentives to increase their portfolio size, motivating them to maximize their debt capacity and risk default. In essence, this is a modeling device to introduce leverage heterogeneity so that a fraction of firms default and the rest remain solvent.

The setting described in the model is most relevant for scenarios where the asset market is relatively thin, leaving the possibility for cash-in-the-market pricing. I draw on anecdotal evidence from the 2007–09 financial crisis to motivate the model's setup and main mechanism. Firms in the model can be thought of as large broker–dealers, hedge funds, or commercial banks with the expertise to participate in a relatively specialized market, like, for example, the market for MBS. The lenders can be thought of as money market funds and regular bond investors catering to these firms financing needs. Arguably, money market funds and regular bond investors would not have the same expertise as broker–dealers or specialized hedge funds to purchase these types of assets. Moreover, it is natural to think that the initial capital committed to a thin market is relatively small compared with the amount of capital held by regular cash investors, thus making firm capital relevant. In this setting, future fire sales create incentives for firms to hold on to their liquidity to take advantage of them.

The main mechanism of the model consists of a group of firms reducing their participation in a risky asset market in anticipation of a future price discount. In one of the model's extensions, when agents do not anticipate the full extent of the cash-in-the-market pricing, firms' initial participation is increased and the severity of the fire sale is uncertain. This involves a larger price discount and potentially more defaults. Anecdotal evidence from market participants and regulators suggests that in the 2008 crisis elements of both models were present: a fraction of agents hoarding capital in anticipation of future discounts and uncertainty to the extent of the price decline upon default. Compared to the original model, a mixture of the two set ups would prescribe a smaller initial discount, a larger fire sale, and potentially more defaults, arguably making the stay exemption regime less desirable.

This paper shows how exemption from automatic stay can distort incentives in some specific settings.

When highly levered firms participate in a relatively illiquid market, prices can deviate from fundamentals, altering firms' decisions and the total costs of default. Though this paper cannot completely resolve the issue whether stay or stay exemption is an optimal bankruptcy regime, it does give insights as to how firms' behavior would change under different regulatory settings when fire sales are a prime concern.

# References

Acharya, V., Shin, H. and Yorulmazer, T. (2011), 'Crisis resolution and bank liquidity', *Review of Financial Studies* **24**(6), 2166–2205.

Acharya, V. and Skeie, D. (2011), 'A model of liquidity hoarding and term premia in inter-bank markets', *Journal of Monetary Economics* **58**(5), 436–447.

Adrian, T., Colla, P. and Shin, H. S. (2012), Which financial frictions? parsing the evidence from the financial crisis of 2007-9, *in* 'NBER Macroeconomics Annual 2012, Volume 27', University of Chicago Press.

Allen, F. and Gale, D. (1994), 'Limited market participation and volatility of asset prices', *The American Economic Review* pp. 933–955.

Allen, F. and Gale, D. (1998), 'Optimal financial crises', *The Journal of Finance* **53**(4), 1245–1284.

Allen, F. and Gale, D. (2005), 'From cash-in-the-market pricing to financial fragility', *Journal of the European Economic Association* **3**(2-3), 535–546.

Antinolfi, G., Carapella, F., Kahn, C., Martin, A., Mills, D. and Nosal, E. (2012), Repos, fire sales, and bankruptcy policy, Technical report, Working Paper, Federal Reserve Bank of Chicago.

Bolton, P. and Oehmke, M. (2011), Should derivatives be privileged in bankruptcy?, Technical report, National Bureau of Economic Research.

Brunnermeier, M. and Pedersen, L. (2009), 'Market liquidity and funding liquidity', *Review of Financial studies* **22**(6), 2201–2238.

Cleveland, H., Huertas, T. and Strauber, R. (1985), *Citibank, 1812-1970*, Harvard University Press Cambridge, MA.

Copeland, A., Martin, A. and Walker, M. (2011), 'Repo runs: Evidence from the tri-party repo market', *New York Federal Reserve Bank Staff Report* **506**.

Diamond, D. W. and Rajan, R. G. (2011), 'Fear of fire sales, illiquidity seeking, and credit freezes', *The Quarterly Journal of Economics* **126**(2), 557–591.

Duffie, D. (1996), 'Special repo rates', *Journal of Finance* **51**(2), 493–526.

Duffie, D. (2010), 'Presidential address: Asset price dynamics with slow-moving capital', *The Journal of Finance* **65**(4), 1237–1267.

Duffie, D. and Skeel, D. (2012), A dialogue on the costs and benefits of automatic stays for derivatives and repurchase agreements, *in* K. Scott and B. Taylor, eds, 'Bankruptcy Not Bailout: A Special Chapter 14', Hoover Institution Press.

Eisfeldt, A. and Rampini, A. (2009), 'Leasing, ability to repossess, and debt capacity', *Review of Financial Studies* **22**(4), 1621–1657.

Fostel, A. and Geanakoplos, J. (2011), Endogenous leverage: Var and beyond, Technical report, Cowles Foundation for Research in Economics, Yale University.

Geanakoplos, J. (2010), 'The Leverage Cycle', *NBER Macroeconomics Annual 2009* **24**, 1–65.

Gorton, G. and Metrick, A. (2012), 'Securitized banking and the run on repo', *Journal of Financial Economics* **104**(3), 425–451.

Gromb, D. and Vayanos, D. (2002), 'Equilibrium and welfare in markets with financially constrained arbitrageurs', *Journal of financial Economics* **66**(2), 361–407.

He, Z., Khang, I. and Krishnamurthy, A. (2010), 'Balance sheet adjustments during the 2008 crisis', *IMF Economic Review* **58**(1), 118–156.

He, Z. and Krishnamurthy, A. (2012), 'A model of capital and crises', *The Review of Economic Studies* **79**(2), 735–777.

Holmstrom, B. and Tirole, J. (1997), 'Financial intermediation, loanable funds, and the real sector', *the Quarterly Journal of economics* **112**(3), 663–691.

Infante, S. (2013), Screening through margins: A model of repo lending, Technical report, Working Paper, Federal Reserve Board.

Kiyotaki, N. and Moore, J. (1997), 'Credit cycles', *The Journal of Political Economy* **105**(2), 211–248.

Krishnamurthy, A. (2010), 'Amplification mechanisms in liquidity crises', *American Economic Journal: Macroeconomics* **2**(3), 1–30.

Krishnamurthy, A., Nagel, S. and Orlov, D. (2012), Sizing up repo, Technical report, National Bureau of Economic Research.

Martin, A., Skeie, D., Thadden, V. et al. (2012), 'Repo runs', *New York Federal Reserve Bank Staff Report* (444).

Oehmke, M. (2013), 'Liquidating illiquid collateral', *Journal of Economic Theory* .

Roe, M. J. (2011), 'The derivatives market's payment priorities as financial crisis accelerator', *Stanford Law Review* **63**(3), 539.

Shleifer, A. and Vishny, R. (1992), 'Liquidation values and debt capacity: A market equilibrium approach', *The Journal of Finance* **47**(4), 1343–1366.

Shleifer, A. and Vishny, R. (1997), 'The Limits of Arbitrage', *Journal of Finance* **52**(1), 35–55.

Shleifer, A. and Vishny, R. (2011), 'Fire sales in finance and macroeconomics', *Journal of Economic Perspectives* **25**(1), 29–48.

Skeel, D. (2001), *Debt's dominion: A history of bankruptcy law in America*, Princeton University Press.

Skeel, D. and Jackson, T. (2012), 'Transaction Consistency and the New Finance in Bankruptcy', *Colum. L. Rev.* **112**.

Stein, J. (2012), 'Monetary policy as financial stability regulation', *The Quarterly Journal of Economics* **127**(1), 57–95.

Stein, J. (2013), 'The fire-sales problem and securities financing transactions'.
   **URL:** *http://www.federalreserve.gov/newsevents/speech/stein20131004a.htm*

# Appendix

*Proof of Proposition* 1:

The analysis of firms optimal behavior can be simply seen by splitting the problem in two. First, consider parameters such that firms optimally choose to take on a safe strategy. This involves solving their investment and financing problem imposing one additional restriction: $I_0^u + \varphi_0 C^L Q_0 \leq \eta C^L Q_0 + A^I - A_0$, i.e. $(Q_0, A_0, I_0^u, \varphi_0) \in N^{\mathcal{S}}$. This condition is more restrictive than the firms capital requirements since $S > C^L$.

Therefore, the safe firms optimization lagrangian takes the following form,

$$
\begin{aligned}
\mathcal{L} = & (\overline{C} + b)Q_0 + A^I - A_0 - I_0^u - \varphi_0 C^{LL} Q_0 + \mu_B(\varphi_0 C^{LL} Q_0 + I_0^u + A_0 - SQ_0) + \\
& \mu_D(\eta C^L Q_0 + A^I - A_0 - I_0^u - \varphi_0 C^{LL} Q_0) + \mu_A(A^I - A_0) + \mu_\varphi(\overline{\varphi} - \varphi_0),
\end{aligned}
$$

note that $A_0 + I_0^u$ appear together in all expression except for the restriction on the firm's dry powder. Ignoring the dry powder restriction, calling $H = A_0 + I_0^u$, and taking FOC gives,

$$\frac{\partial \mathcal{L}}{\partial Q_0} = \overline{C} + b - \varphi_0 C^{LL} + \mu_B(\varphi_0 C^{LL} - S) + \mu_D(\eta C^L - \varphi_0 C^{LL}) \le 0,$$

$$\frac{\partial \mathcal{L}}{\partial H} = -1 + \mu_B - \mu_D \le 0,$$

$$\frac{\partial \mathcal{L}}{\partial \varphi_0} = -C^{LL} Q_0 + \mu_B C^{LL} Q_0 - \mu_D C^{LL} Q_0 - \mu_{\varphi_0} \le 0.$$

**Case $H^* > 0$ & $Q_0^* > 0$:** Implies $\mu_B = \mu_D + 1 > 0$, thus the budget constraint is active. Replacing $\mu_B$ in the first equation gives,

$$\mu_D = \frac{\overline{C} + b - S}{S - \eta C^L},$$

thus if $S < \overline{C} + b$ (since $S > \eta C^L$ by assumption) the firm takes on the maximum amount of leverage: $I_0^{u*} + \varphi_0^* C^{LL} Q_0^* = \eta C^L Q_0^* + A^I - A_0^*$. Together with the budget constraint solves for $Q_0^*$. If $S = \overline{C} + b$, then the amount of debt and asset purchase are undetermined. Note that in both of these sub cases $\varphi_0^*$ is not pinned down.

**Case $H^* > 0$ & $Q_0^* = 0$:** Implies $\mu_B = \mu_D + 1$, thus the budget constraint is active and $H^* = 0$ leading to a contradiction.

**Case $H^* = 0$:** Implies $\mu_B < \mu_D + 1$ which from the final equation implies $\varphi_0^* = 0$. The budget constraint implies $Q_0^* = 0$ and the refinancing condition is slack. Using the first FOC, and noting that $\mu_B < 1$, gives $\mu_B S > \overline{C} + b$, thus $S > \overline{C} + b$ pinning down the firm's strategies.

Turning to the risky firm, using equation (3), the price of risky debt alters the value of the firms risky asset position to

$$C^D(\varphi_0) = (\alpha C^H + (1 - \alpha)(\varphi_0 C^L + (1 - \varphi_0)\lambda C^L)).$$

The optimization's lagrangian takes the following form,

$$\mathcal{L} = (C^D(\varphi_0) + b)Q_0 + (\alpha + (1 - \alpha)\lambda)(A^I - A_0) - \varphi_0 C^{LL} Q_0 - I_0^u + \mu_A(A^I - A_0) +$$
$$\mu_B(\varphi_0 C^{LL} Q_0 + I_0^u + A_0 - SQ_0) + \mu_D(\eta(SQ_0 + A^I - A_0) - I_0^u - \varphi_0 C^{LL} Q_0) + \mu_\varphi(\overline{\varphi} - \varphi_0).$$

Taking FOC gives,

$$\frac{\partial \mathcal{L}}{\partial Q_0} = C^D(\varphi_0) + b - \varphi_0 C^{LL} + \mu_B(\varphi_0 C^{LL} - S) + \mu_D(\eta S - \varphi_0 C^{LL}) \le 0,$$

$$\frac{\partial \mathcal{L}}{\partial I_0^u} = -1 + \mu_B - \mu_D \le 0,$$

$$\frac{\partial \mathcal{L}}{\partial \varphi_0} = (1 - \alpha)(1 - \lambda)C^L Q_0 - C^{LL} Q_0 + \mu_B C^{LL} Q_0 - \mu_D C^{LL} Q_0 - \mu_{\varphi_0} \le 0,$$

$$\frac{\partial \mathcal{L}}{\partial A_0} = -(\alpha + (1 - \alpha)\lambda) - \mu_A + \mu_B - \eta\mu_D \le 0.$$

Since this part of the proof characterizes the optimal strategy of a levered firm consider the case when $\mu_D > 0$.

**Case $\mu_D > 0$ & $I_u > 0$:** Implies $\mu_B = \mu_D + 1$ which from the final two equations implies $\mu_{\varphi_0}, \mu_A > 0$. Given that the budget constraint is active and $A_0^* = A^I$, necessarily $Q_0^* > 0$. Replacing $\mu_B$ in the first equation gives,

$$\mu_D = \frac{C^D(\overline{\varphi}) + b - S}{S(1 - \eta)},$$

thus if $C^D + b > S$, the firm takes on maximal leverage $I_0^{*u} + \overline{\varphi} C^{LL} Q_0 = \eta S Q_0$. Together with the budget constraint solves for $Q_0^*$.

**Case $\mu_D > 0$ & $I_u = 0$:** The capital requirement restriction implies $\varphi_0 C^{LL} Q_0 = \eta(SQ_0 + A^I - A_0)$, therefore in the very

39

least $\overline{\varphi}C^{LL} \geq \eta S$. But from assumption A1 and $S > C^L$ it can be deduced that $\eta S > \overline{\varphi}C^{LL}$, leading to a contradiction.

It must be verified that the firm would in fact default in the down state, that is the firm cannot roll over it's debt. From equation (5) the maximum firm can raise after a bad outcome is $\eta C^L Q_0 + (A^I - A_0)$. From equation (3) and the firms default costs, risky unsecured debt is

$$\alpha F_0^u = I_0^u - (1 - \alpha)\left((\varphi_0 C^L + \lambda(1 - \varphi_0)C^L)Q_0 + \lambda(A_0^I - A_0) - \varphi_0 C^{LL}Q_0\right),$$

then for firms to default $F_0^u + \varphi_0 C^{LL} Q_0 > \eta C^L Q_0 + (A^I - A_0)$ which is equivalent to,

$$I_0^u + \varphi_0 C^{LL} Q_0 > (\alpha\eta + (1 - \alpha)[\varphi_0 + \lambda(1 - \varphi_0)]) C^L Q_0 + (\alpha + \lambda(1 - \alpha))(A^I - A_0).$$

Under assumption A1, considering the optimal strategy $A^* = A^I$, and $S > C^L$ this inequality holds.

Pinning down both types of firms optimal strategies and payoffs, the threshold function $b^*(S)$ must be characterized to determine when firms take a risky or safe strategy. In effect, for risky firms to have a positive payoff it is necessary to consider $S \leq C^D(\overline{\varphi}) + b$, with $b > 0$, giving the first two restrictions for $b^*(S)$. In that price range, the optimal strategy for safe firms is to increase their debt capacity till they can roll over their debt. Thus, a risky strategy will be preferred if,

$$\frac{C^D(\overline{\varphi}) + b - S}{S(1 - \eta)} \geq \frac{\overline{C} + b - S}{S - \eta C^L} \iff$$

$$b \geq \frac{(\overline{C} - S)S(1 - \eta) - (C^D(\overline{\varphi}) - S)(S - \eta C^L)}{\eta(S - C^L)} := b'(S),$$

defining $b^*(S) = \max\{0, S - C^D(\overline{\varphi}), b'(S)\}$, for $b \geq b^*(S)$ firms will choose risky strategies, completing the proof.

∎

*Proof of Proposition 2:*

The analysis of firms' optimal behavior is similar to the stay regime, which can be simply seen by splitting the problem in two. First consider parameters such that firms optimally choose to take on a safe strategy. This involves solving their investment and financing problem on additional restriction: $I_0^u + \varphi_0 S^L Q_0 \leq \eta S^L Q_0 + A^I - A_0$, i.e. $(Q_0, A_0, I_0^u, \varphi_0) \in N^{S\mathcal{E}}$. This condition is more restrictive than the firms capital requirements since $S^L > C^L$.

Therefore, the safe firms optimization lagrangian takes the following form,

$$\begin{aligned}
\mathcal{L} &= (\overline{C} + b)Q_0 + (A^I - A_0) + (1 - \alpha)(C^L - S^L)\left(\frac{\eta S^L Q_0 + (A^I - A_0) - I_0^u - \varphi_0 S^L Q_0}{S^L(1 - \eta)}\right) - \\
&\quad \varphi_0 S^L Q_0 - I_0^u + \mu_B(\varphi_0 S^L Q_0 + I_0^u + A_0 - SQ_0) + \mu_A(A^I - A_0) + \mu_\varphi(\overline{\varphi} - \varphi) + \\
&\quad \mu_D(\eta S^L Q_0 + A^I - A_0 - I_0^u - \varphi_0 S^L Q_0),
\end{aligned}$$

note that $A_0 + I_0^u$ appear together in all expressions except for the restriction on the firm's dry powder. Ignoring the dry powder restriction, calling $H = A_0 + I_0^u$, and taking FOC gives,

$$\begin{aligned}
\frac{\partial\mathcal{L}}{\partial Q_0} &= \overline{C} + b - \varphi_0 S^L + (1 - \alpha)\left(\frac{C^L - S^L}{S^L(1 - \eta)}\right)(\eta - \varphi_0)S^L + \mu_B(\varphi_0 S^L - S) + \mu_D(\eta - \varphi_0)S^L \leq 0, \\
\frac{\partial\mathcal{L}}{\partial H} &= -1 - (1 - \alpha)\left(\frac{C^L - S^L}{S^L(1 - \eta)}\right) + \mu_B - \mu_D \leq 0, \\
\frac{\partial\mathcal{L}}{\partial \varphi_0} &= -S^L Q_0 - (1 - \alpha)\left(\frac{C^L - S^L}{S^L(1 - \eta)}\right)S^L Q_0 + \mu_B S^L Q_0 - \mu_D S^L Q_0 - \mu_\varphi \leq 0.
\end{aligned}$$

**Case $H^* > 0$ & $Q_0^* > 0$:** Implies $\mu_B = 1 + (1 - \alpha)\left(\frac{C^L - S^L}{S^L(1 - \eta)}\right) + \mu_D > 0$, thus the budget constraint is active since $S^L \leq C^L$.

40

Replacing $\mu_B$ in the first equation gives,

$$\mu_D = \frac{\overline{C} + b - S + (1-\alpha)\left(\frac{C^L - S^L}{S^L(1-\eta)}\right)(\eta S^L - S)}{S - \eta S^L},$$

thus if

$$S\left(1 + (1-\alpha)\left(\frac{C^L - S^L}{S^L(1-\eta)}\right)\right) < \overline{C} + b + (1-\alpha)\left(\frac{C^L - S^L}{S^L(1-\eta)}\right)\eta S^L,$$

since $S > S^L$ by assumption the firm takes on the maximum amount of leverage: $I_0^{u*} + \varphi_0^* S^L Q_0^* + A_0^* = \eta S^L Q_0^* + A^I$. Together with the budget constraint solves for $Q_0^*$. If $S$ is such that $\mu_D = 0$, then the amount of debt and asset purchase are undetermined, and the above inequality is with equality and characterizes $S(S^L, b)$. Note that in both cases $\varphi_0^*$ is not pinned down.

**Case $H^* > 0$ & $Q_0^* = 0$:** Implies $\mu_B = 1 + (1-\alpha)\left(\frac{C^L - S^L}{S^L(1-\eta)}\right) + \mu_D$. Since $C^L \geq S^L$ it follows that the budget constraint is active and $H^* = 0$, leading to a contradiction.

**Case $H^* = 0$:** Implies $\mu_B < 1 + (1-\alpha)\left(\frac{C^L - S^L}{S^L - \eta S^L}\right) + \mu_D$ which from the final equation implies that $\varphi_0^* = 0$. The budget constraint implies $Q_0^* = 0$ and that the refinancing condition is slack: $\mu_D = 0$. Noting that $\mu_B < 1 + (1-\alpha)\left(\frac{C^L - S^L}{S^L(1-\eta)}\right)$ the first FOC gives,

$$\mu_B S > \overline{C} + b + (1-\alpha)\left(\frac{C^L - S^L}{S^L(1-\eta)}\right)\eta S^L,$$

therefore $S > S^{BE}(S^L, b)$.

Turning to the risky firm, using equation (4) the price of risky debt alters the value of the firms risky asset position to,

$$C^D(\varphi_0, S^L) = (\alpha C^H + (1-\alpha)(\varphi_0 S^L + (1-\varphi_0)\lambda C^L)).$$

Note that the lower bound on $S^L > \lambda C^L$ is to ensure that the firms decides to first exhaust it's secured funding before it raises unsecured funding. The optimization's lagrangian takes the following form,

$$\begin{aligned}
\mathcal{L} &= (C^D(\varphi_0, S^L) + b)Q_0 + (\alpha + (1-\alpha)\lambda)(A^I - A_0) - \varphi_0 S^L Q_0 - I_0^u + \mu_A(A^I - A_0) + \\
&\quad \mu_B(\varphi_0 S^L Q_0 + I_0^u + A_0 - SQ_0) + \mu_D(\eta(SQ_0 + (A^I - A_0)) - I_0^u - \varphi_0 S^L Q_0) + \mu_\varphi(\overline{\varphi} - \varphi_0).
\end{aligned}$$

Taking FOC we have,

$$\begin{aligned}
\frac{\partial \mathcal{L}}{\partial Q_0} &= C^D(\varphi_0, S^L) + b - \varphi_0 S^L + \mu_B(\varphi_0 S^L - S) + \mu_D(\eta S - \varphi_0 S^L) \leq 0, \\
\frac{\partial \mathcal{L}}{\partial I_0^u} &= -1 + \mu_B - \mu_D \leq 0, \\
\frac{\partial \mathcal{L}}{\partial \varphi_0} &= (1-\alpha)(S^L - \lambda C^L)Q_0 - S^L Q_0 + \mu_B S^L Q_0 - \mu_D S^L Q_0 - \mu_\varphi 0 \leq 0, \\
\frac{\partial \mathcal{L}}{\partial A_0} &= -(\alpha + (1-\alpha)\lambda) - \mu_A + \mu_B - \eta \mu_D \leq 0,
\end{aligned}$$

since $S^L > \lambda C^L$ the arguments are identical as in the proof of proposition 2. Thus the optimal strategies and final payoffs take the same form by replacing $C^D(\varphi)$ by $C^D(\varphi, S^L)$, $C^{LL}$ by $S^L$ and $C^L$ by $S^L$ in part of the FOC for $\varphi_0$.

It must be verified that the firm would in fact default in the down state, that is the firm cannot roll over it's debt. From equation (6) the maximum a firm can raise after a bad outcome is $\eta S^L Q_0 + (A^I - A_0)$. From equation (4) and the firms default costs, risky unsecured debt is

$$\alpha F_0^u = I_0^u - (1-\alpha)\left(\lambda(1-\varphi_0)C^L Q_0 + \lambda(A_0^I - A_0)\right),$$

therefore the default condition is $F_0^u + \varphi_0 S^L Q_0 > \eta S^L Q_0 + (A^I - A_0)$ which is equivalent to,

$$I_0^u + \varphi_0 S^L Q_0 > \left(\alpha \eta S^L + (1 - \alpha)[\varphi_0 S^L + \lambda(1 - \varphi_0)C^L]\right) Q_0 + (\alpha + \lambda(1 - \alpha))(A^I - A_0).$$

Assuming A1, considering the optimal strategy $A_0 = A^I$, and $S > S^L > \lambda C^L$ this inequality holds.

Pinning down both types of firms optimal strategies and payoff, the threshold function $b^{**}(S, S^L)$ must be characterized to determine when firms in fact take a risky or safe strategy. To do so, it must be that firms with a private benefit $b$ prefer the risky strategy above both safe alternatives; where one of the safe strategies gives them a potential fire sale profit. In case the optimal safe strategy is to maintain dry powder the following inequality must hold,

$$\frac{(C^D(\overline{\varphi}, S^L) + b - S)A^I}{S(1 - \eta)} + A^I \geq (1 - \alpha)\left(\frac{C^L - S^L}{S^L(1 - \eta)}\right)A^I + A^I \iff$$

$$b \geq S\left[(1 - \alpha)\left(\frac{C^L - S^L}{S^L}\right) - \left(\frac{C^D(\overline{\varphi}, S^L) - S}{S}\right)\right] := b''(S, S^L)$$

In case the optimal safe strategy is to increase debt capacity till the firm can roll over it's debt, firms will choose a risky strategy if

$$\frac{(C^D(\overline{\varphi}, S^L) + b - S)A^I}{S(1 - \eta)} + A^I \geq \frac{(\overline{C} + b - S)A^I}{S - \eta S^L} + A^I \iff$$

$$b \geq \frac{(\overline{C} - S)S(1 - \eta) - (C^D(\overline{\varphi}, S^L) - S)(S - \eta S^L)}{\eta(S - S^L)} := b'''(S, S^L),$$

defining $b^{**}(S, S^L) = \max\{0, b''(S, S^L), b'''(S, S^L)\}$, for $b \geq b^{**}(S, S^L)$ firms will choose risky strategies, completing the proof.

∎

*Proof of Theorem 1:*

With the conjectured equilibrium has $S = \overline{C}$, it is clear that non private benefit firms will adopt a safe strategy since otherwise their payoff would be lower than their initial endowment. For these firms, proposition 1 states that their demand is undetermined $Q^{undet} \in [0, A^I/(\overline{C} - \eta C^L))$, and final payoff is their initial endowment.

Private benefit firms have to be motivated to take on the risky strategy. From the proof of proposition 1, the condition $b > b^*(\overline{C})$ ensures these firms take risky strategies. This amounts to having,

$$b > (\overline{C} - C^D(\overline{\varphi}))\frac{\overline{C} - \eta C^L}{\eta(\overline{C} - C^L)} := b^*,$$

since this is more restrictive than $\overline{C} - C^D(\overline{\varphi})$ and $b^* > 0$. Thus if $b > b^*$ private benefit firms will adopt a risky strategy.

Integrating over firms demand and imposing market clearing gives,

$$\frac{A^I \theta}{\overline{C}(1 - \eta)} + \overline{Q}^{NPB} = K,$$

which holds for all $\overline{Q}^{NPB} \in \left[0, \frac{A^I(1 - \theta)}{\overline{C} - \eta C^L}\right)$, pinning down the supply interval in which the equilibrium holds.

∎

*Proof of Theorem 2:*

I conjecture that the equilibrium for relatively low levels of asset supply has firms adopt DP strategies. The fire sale premium for these firms must be relatively large. In the conjectured equilibrium, the relation between the first and second period price stems from market clearing in the refinancing period (imposing the parameterization of $\theta$ from A2) , i.e.

$$\overline{\varphi}\frac{A^I\theta}{S(1-\eta)} = \frac{A^I(1-\theta)}{S^L(1-\eta)} \implies S^L = \frac{1-\theta}{\overline{\varphi}\theta}S = \frac{C^L}{\overline{C}}S := \phi S,$$

that is, in this setting, the initial gross return of the asset is equal to the gross fire sale return. If $S > S^{BE}(S^L, 0)$ non private benefit firms will refrain from investing in the initial period. This is equivalent to,

$$1 + \frac{(1-\alpha)(C^L - S^L)}{S^L(1-\eta)} > \frac{\overline{C}}{S} + \frac{(1-\alpha)(C^L - S^L)}{S^L(1-\eta)}\frac{\eta S^L}{S},$$

imposing the relationship between gross returns gives,

$$(1-\alpha)(1-\eta\phi) > (1-\eta), \tag{18}$$

which, by replacing $\phi$, is condition A3. Thus, non private benefit firms opt to only invest in the refinancing period for relatively low levels of asset supply. To conclude that private benefit firms take on risky strategies, it is necessary to determine the value of $b^{**}$ such that $b^{**} \geq b^{**}(S, S^L)$ for all $S$ and $S^L$ in the conjectured equilibrium. From the proof of Proposition 2 there are two possible expressions for $b^{**}$. The first is so that private benefit firms prefer risky strategies over investing in a dry powder strategy, and the other is so that private benefit firms prefer risky strategies over investing with low levels of debt. Imposing the conjectured equilibrium gives,

$$b''(S) = (1-\alpha)\frac{C^L}{\phi} + \alpha S - C^D(\overline{\varphi}, \phi S),$$

$$b'''(S) = \frac{\overline{C}(1-\eta) - C^D(\overline{\varphi}, \phi S)(1-\phi\eta)}{\eta(1-\phi)} + S.$$

Therefore, choosing private benefits such that $b^{**} > \max\{b''(S), b'''(S)\}$ for all $S$ in the conjectured equilibrium, private benefit firms will adopt a risky strategy.[40]

Having pinned down private and non private benefit firms strategies, market clearing in the first period is expressed as,

$$\frac{A^I\theta}{S(1-\eta)} = K.$$

It must be verified $S^L > \lambda C^L$ for proposition 2 to hold. From market clearing and $S^L = \phi S$, this equates to

$$\lambda K < \frac{A^I\theta}{\overline{C}(1-\eta)}.$$

To ensure that the fire sale isn't too low it is sufficient to prove that $K^S_{max}$ satisfies this bound, i.e.

$$(1-\lambda)\left(\frac{1}{\phi}-\eta\right) > \lambda(1-\eta)\overline{\varphi}.$$

This inequality is precisely assumption A4. Finally, to ensure the existence of $K^M$ in which firms enter a DP-mixing equilibrium, is must be shown that there exists a price low enough for non private benefit firms to mix between safe and risky strategies. The mixing condition (equation (9)) gives,

$$\alpha\frac{A\theta}{K(1-\eta)} + (1-\alpha)\overline{C} = C^D\left(\overline{\varphi}, \phi\frac{A\theta}{K(1-\eta)}\right),$$

---

[40] For a large set of primitive parameters of the model, the above expressions for $b''(S)$ and $b'''(S)$ are increasing in $S$. Thus, imposing private benefits to be equal to these functions when $S = \overline{C}$ (which coincides with the stay regime private benefits) will ensure the correct behavior.

which defines
$$K^M = \frac{A\theta}{\overline{C}(1-\eta)} + \frac{(1-\overline{\varphi})(1-\lambda)C^L}{\alpha\overline{C} - (1-\alpha)[\overline{\varphi} + (1-\overline{\varphi})(1-\lambda)]C^L}\frac{A\theta}{\overline{C}(1-\eta)}.$$

Thus, $K^M$ must be smaller than $K^S_{max}$, which is assumption A5.

The above proof ensures that for $K \in [K^S_{min}, K^M]$ non private benefit firms adopt a DP strategies. For levels of supply greater than $K^M$, non private benefit firms mix between risky and safe strategies. Therefore market clearing in $t = 1$ takes on the following form,

$$\overline{\varphi}\frac{A^I(\theta + \xi(1-\theta))}{S(1-\eta)} = \frac{A^I(1-\xi)(1-\theta)}{S^L(1-\eta)} \iff S^L = \frac{(1-\theta)(1-\xi)}{\overline{\varphi}(\theta + \xi(1-\theta))}S := \hat{\phi}(\xi)S,$$

where $\xi$ is the fraction of non private benefit firms that take on risky strategies. Note that $\xi = 0$ for $K = K^M$, $\hat{\phi}(0) = \phi$, and $\hat{\phi}(\xi)$ is decreasing in $\xi$. Given the conjectured strategies, market clearing in the initial period is given by,

$$\frac{A(\theta + \xi(1-\theta))}{S(1-\eta)} = K,$$

and non private benefit firms mixing condition (equation (9)) is equivalent to,

$$(1-\alpha)\left(\frac{C^L}{S^L} - 1\right) = \frac{C^D(\overline{\varphi}, S^L)}{S} - 1 \iff$$
$$S\left(\alpha - (1-\alpha)\frac{(1-\theta)(1-\xi)}{(\theta + \xi(1-\theta))}\right) = \alpha C^H + (1-\alpha)(1-\overline{\varphi})\lambda C^L - (1-\alpha)\overline{\varphi}\frac{(\theta + \xi(1-\theta))}{(1-\theta)(1-\xi)}C^L.$$

To verify that this in fact will constitute an equilibrium, it must be checked that private benefit and non private benefit firms adopt the corresponding DP-mixing strategies. This analysis is equivalent to the DP strategy analysis, replacing $\phi$ with $\hat{\phi}(\xi)$ for conditions stemming from equation (18), $S^L > \lambda C^L$, $b''$, and $b'''$. Note that conditions in equation (18) and $b'''$ are relaxed as $\xi$ increases, which hold for $\xi = 0$. Conditions stemming from $S^L > \lambda C^L$ and $b''$ become tighter as $\xi$ increases, thus there exists a $\xi^*$ such that for all $\xi < \xi^*$ both these inequalities continue to hold. Defining $K^{S\mathcal{E}}_{max}$ as the minimum between $K^S_{max}$ and the asset supply such that the fraction of mixing firms is equal to $\xi^*$, ensures that for all $K \in (K^M, K^{S\mathcal{E}}_{max})$ firms enter a DP-mixing equilibrium, completing the proof.

**Lemma 1.** *Under the assumptions of Theorem 2, comparative statics of the Dry Powder equilibrium for $K \in [K^S_{min}, K^M]$ depend on the equilibrium equation*
$$S = \frac{A^I\theta}{K(1-\eta)},$$
*with $S^L = \frac{1-\theta}{\overline{\varphi}\theta}S$.*

*Comparative statics of the Dry Powder Mixing equilibrium for $K \in (K^M, K^{S\mathcal{E}}_{max}]$ depend on the equilibrium equations,*

$$T_1 = \frac{A^I p}{K(1-\eta)} - S = 0,$$
$$T_2 = \Gamma(C^H, C^L, \alpha, \overline{\varphi}, \lambda) - (1-\alpha)\overline{\varphi}\frac{p}{1-p}C^L - S\left(\alpha - (1-\alpha)\frac{1-p}{p}\right) = 0,$$

*where $\Gamma(C^H, C^L, \alpha, \overline{\varphi}, \lambda) = \alpha C^H + (1-\alpha)(1-\overline{\varphi})\lambda C^L$ and $p = \theta + \xi(1-\theta) > \theta$ with $S^L = \frac{1-p}{\overline{\varphi}p}S$. If $\theta > 1 - \alpha$, for all parameters $x \in \{A^I, K, \eta, \lambda, \alpha, C^H, C^L\}$ either*

$$\frac{\partial T_1}{\partial x} = 0 \quad and \quad sgn\left(\frac{\frac{\partial p}{\partial x}}{\frac{\partial S}{\partial x}}\right) = sgn\left(\frac{\frac{\partial T_2}{\partial x}}{\frac{\partial T_2}{\partial x}}\right),$$

with $sgn\left(\frac{\partial S^L}{\partial x}\right) = sgn\left(-\frac{\partial T_2}{\partial x}\right)$, or

$$\frac{\partial T_2}{\partial x} = 0 \quad and \quad sgn\left(\frac{\frac{\partial p}{\partial x}}{\frac{\partial S}{\partial x}}\right) = sgn\left(\frac{-\frac{\partial T_1}{\partial x}}{\frac{\partial T_1}{\partial x}}\right),$$

with $sgn\left(\frac{\partial S^L}{\partial x}\right) = sgn\left(\frac{\partial T_1}{\partial x}\right)$

*Proof of Lemma 1*

The first part of the Lemma is direct from the DP equilibrium characterization of Theorem 2 as well as the equilibrium equations $T_1, T_2$ for the DP Mixing equilibrium. Holding $\theta$ fixed, by inspection it can be appreciated that for any change in $x \in \{A^I, K, \eta, \lambda, \alpha, C^H, C^L\}$ results in either $\frac{\partial T_1}{\partial x} = 0$ or $\frac{\partial T_2}{\partial x} = 0$. Using the implicit theorem I can study how equilibrium variables $S$ and $p$ change with underlying parameters.

$$\begin{aligned}
\frac{\partial T_1}{\partial p} &= \frac{A}{K(1-\eta)} > 0, \\
\frac{\partial T_1}{\partial S} &= -1 < 0, \\
\frac{\partial T_2}{\partial p} &= -(1-\alpha)\left(\frac{\overline{\varphi}C^L}{(1-p)^2} + \frac{S}{p^2}\right) < 0, \\
\frac{\partial T_2}{\partial S} &= (1-\alpha)\frac{1-p}{p} - \alpha < 0,
\end{aligned}$$

where the sign of the last partial derivative stems from the fact that $\theta > 1 - \alpha$, for $\xi = 0\,(1-\alpha)\frac{1-p}{p} < \alpha$, and $\frac{1-p}{p}$ decreases with $p$. Denoting

$$M = \begin{bmatrix} \frac{\partial T_1}{\partial p} & \frac{\partial T_1}{\partial S} \\ \frac{\partial T_2}{\partial p} & \frac{\partial T_2}{\partial S} \end{bmatrix} = \begin{bmatrix} \frac{A}{K(1-\eta)} & -1 \\ -(1-\alpha)\left(\frac{\overline{\varphi}C^L}{(1-p)^2} + \frac{S}{p^2}\right) & (1-\alpha)\frac{1-p}{p} - \alpha \end{bmatrix}.$$

Note that $det(M) < 0$. Thus applying the implicit function theorem,

$$\begin{pmatrix} \frac{\partial p}{\partial x} \\ \frac{\partial S}{\partial x} \end{pmatrix} = -M^{-1}\begin{pmatrix} \frac{\partial T_1}{\partial x} \\ \frac{\partial T_2}{\partial x} \end{pmatrix} = \frac{-1}{det(M)}\begin{bmatrix} (1-\alpha)\frac{1-p}{p} - \alpha & 1 \\ (1-\alpha)\left(\frac{\overline{\varphi}C^L}{(1-p)^2} + \frac{S}{p^2}\right) & \frac{A}{K(1-\eta)} \end{bmatrix}\begin{pmatrix} \frac{\partial T_1}{\partial x} \\ \frac{\partial T_2}{\partial x} \end{pmatrix}.$$

Thus, $x \in \{A^I, K, \eta\}$ gives $\frac{\partial T_2}{\partial x} = 0$ and

$$\begin{pmatrix} \frac{\partial p}{\partial x} \\ \frac{\partial S}{\partial x} \end{pmatrix} = \frac{-1}{det(M)}\begin{pmatrix} \left((1-\alpha)\frac{1-p}{p} - \alpha\right)\frac{\partial T_1}{\partial x} \\ (1-\alpha)\left(\frac{\overline{\varphi}C^L}{(1-p)^2} + \frac{S}{p^2}\right)\frac{\partial T_1}{\partial x} \end{pmatrix}.$$

And $x \in \{\lambda, \alpha, C^H, C^L\}$ gives $\frac{\partial T_1}{\partial x} = 0$ and

$$\begin{pmatrix} \frac{\partial p}{\partial x} \\ \frac{\partial S}{\partial x} \end{pmatrix} = \frac{-1}{det(M)}\begin{pmatrix} \frac{\partial T_2}{\partial x} \\ \frac{A}{K(1-\eta)}\frac{\partial T_2}{\partial x} \end{pmatrix}.$$

Finally, note that in both cases of the DP mixing equilibrium

$$\frac{\partial S^L}{\partial x} = \left(\frac{\partial S}{\partial x}\frac{1-p}{p} - \frac{\partial p}{\partial x}\frac{S}{p^2}\right),$$

therefore, in case $\frac{\partial T_2}{\partial x} = 0$ this implies,

$$\frac{\partial S^L}{\partial x} = \frac{-1}{det(M)\overline{\varphi}}\left((1-\alpha)\frac{\overline{\varphi}C^L}{p(1-p)} + \alpha\frac{S}{p^2}\right)\frac{\partial T_1}{\partial x},$$

45

and in case $\frac{\partial T_1}{\partial x} = 0$ this implies,

$$\frac{\partial S^L}{\partial x} = \frac{1}{det(M)\overline{\varphi}} \frac{S}{p} \frac{\partial T_2}{\partial x}.$$